Travers' Rare Coin Investment Strategy

Author Scott A. Travers (l) meets with James A. Baker III, Secretary of the Treasury under President Ronald Reagan. They both attended the Statue of Liberty commemorative coin First Strike Ceremony at West Point, New York. (Photo by Ed Reiter)

Travers' Rare Coin Investment Strategy

Second Edition

Scott A. Travers

PRENTICE
HALL
PRESS

New York   London   Toronto   Sydney   Tokyo

To my parents

The information contained in this book has been compiled based on the past performance of coins. However, past performance is not a guarantee of future performance. Furthermore, no book about coin investment, no matter how technical or complete, can provide for every possible marketplace scenario. You are advised to consult with competent professionals to determine which coins, *if any,* are suitable for you, especially if large sums of money are involved. The author neither warrants nor represents that any reader of this book or follower of any advice contained herein will achieve positive financial results. Consequently, the author disclaims responsibility for any loss, monetary or otherwise, that might occur as a result of the use of any information herein.

Excerpts from *Mark Skousen's Complete Guide to Financial Privacy* are reprinted with the permission of Simon & Schuster, Inc.

All photographs in chapter 6, except where indicated, have been provided courtesy Heritage Capital Corporation.

PRENTICE HALL PRESS
15 Columbus Circle
New York, NY 10023

Library of Congress Cataloging-in-Publication Data

Travers, Scott A.
Travers' rare coin investment strategy.
1. Coins as an investment.   I. Title.   II. Title: Rare coin investment strategy.
CJ81.T74   1990   332.63   89-23226
ISBN 0-13-752965-1

Manufactured in the United States of America

10 9 8 7 6 5 4 3 2 1

Second Edition

Acknowledgments

Credit is due the following persons who were of invaluable assistance: David T. Alexander; Burnett Anderson; Stanley Apfelbaum; Dennis Baker; James E. Bandler; Q. David Bowers; Morris Bram; Walter Breen; Kenneth E. Bressett; Ruthann Brettell; Pedro Collazo-Oliver; William L. Corsa, Sr.; Michael G. DeFalco; George DeWolfe; James DiGeorgia; Beth Deisher; Janet Dore; Martin H. Firman; William Fivaz; Les Fox; Leo Frese; Michael R. Fuljenz; Joel Gabrelow; David L. Ganz; Paul M. Green; Martin E. Haber; David Hall; Kenneth Hallenbeck; James L. Halperin; David C. Harper; George D. Hatie; Michael R. Haynes; Leon Hendrickson; Ed Hipps; Charles Hoskins; David Hunt; Steve Ivy; Donald H. Kagin; George Klabin; Chester L. Krause; Julian Leidman; Mallory J. Lennox; Kevin Lipton; Samuel G. Liss; Andrew P. Lustig; James L. Miller; Warren Mills; Lee S. Minshull; Richard S. Montgomery; Sarah Montague; Bernard Nagengast; William J. Nagle; John Pasciuti; Martin B. Paul; Donn Pearlman; Arnold I. Rady; Ed Reiter; Robert S. Riemer; Edward C. Rochette; Bernard Rome; Joseph H. Rose; Maurice Rosen; Larry Ruff; Margo Russell; Florence M. Schook; Howard Segermark; Michael Sherman; Arlyn G. Sieber; Les Simone; Harvey G. Stack; Michael Standish; Dennis E. Steinmetz; Rick Sundman; Anthony J. Swiatek; Sol Taylor; Michael Toledo; Julius Turoff; Bob Vitt; Bob Wilhite; Douglas A. Winter; and Keith M. Zaner.

Credit is also due the following institutions and corporations: American Numismatic Association Certification Service; Amos Press, Inc.; Coin Dealer Newsletter; Heritage Capital Corporation; Krause Publications, Inc.; Miller Magazines, Inc.; Numismatic Guaranty Corporation of America; Numismatic Literary Guild; Professional Coin Grading Service; Salomon Brothers Inc.; and Western Publishing Company, Inc.

Contents

Foreword

For the past five years, almost anything that smacks of "hard money," "collectibles," or "inflation hedge" has been in a bear market—with the exception of rare coins, many of which have bucked this trend to new highs.

The supply of rare coins has been mopped up by collectors and investors almost as fast as they can come on the market.

These savvy contrarians have discovered one fundamental characteristic that makes these coins so attractive—"they ain't makin' no more of 'em," and much of what comes to light is being socked away by collectors and investors who anticipate the return of inflation.

Unfortunately, however, much of this demand comes from inexperienced and unsophisticated collectors, and it is a temptation for coin dealers to shear the lambs. There is a lot of misinformation, overgrading, overpricing, and fraud in the coin industry. That doesn't mean you should avoid investing in coins—far from it. But it does mean you must be knowledgeable and work with dealers with a long track record of conservative grading and unimpeachable integrity.

Scott Travers is one of these people. His first book, *The Coin Collector's Survival Manual,* was a classic, and this new book bids to outshine his earlier work.

The portfolio of the knowledgeable rare coin investor would probably flourish over the next few years due to collector demand, even if higher inflation doesn't materialize and bring a stampede of inflation-hedge investors out of the woodwork. But if inflation begins to rise again (and I believe it will—in spades), very few investments will have even a remote chance of out-performing a well-selected portfolio of rare coins.

But before you trot off to the nearest coin dealer and grab everything in sight, take advantage of a pro—Scott Travers. He knows what he's talking about.

—HOWARD RUFF

Introduction

In hosting the first two Coin Collectors' Survival Conferences, your author, Scott Travers, has done something unprecedented in the history of coin collecting and investing: he has induced collectors and investors to think very differently about the entire hobby/profession/political football game. Their survival theme is to stay in the game—not necessarily at life-and-death stakes. The participants' recurrent metaphors might just as easily have applied to poker or the stock market.

At coin shows nationwide, the words differ but the tune is the same; the mind-set is that of playing any competitive game. Originally, the goal of collecting was to accumulate the most highly valued game counters and still retain enough money to go on playing; more recently, the goal has increasingly been to get rich quick. Understandably, some players merely break the rules; others are trying to change the rules to get away with having broken them. In this game, dealers were originally resource persons; more recently, many have become collectors' allies—or opponents. The tone of their Triumph Displays at a win resembles the morning-after boasts of poker players and bargain hunters. A collector's or investor's win sounds like, "Look at what I cherrypicked from the auction last night!" A dealer's win may sound something like "You wouldn't *believe* what I just bought for peanuts" or "You know that set everybody said was a white elephant? Well, I just sold it for 50 percent over Trends. . . ."

To call coin collecting and investing a game is not to trivialize it: when the stakes in any game become large enough, players tend more and more to identify it with "real life," the biggest and oldest game of all (especially when they earn their livings at it). Thousands of years before our ancestors learned to talk, the name of the game they all had evolved to play was "Survive in the Jungle." The stakes were life and death, and before your tribe developed appropriate technology (or imported it), you couldn't take much time off to play anything else. Finding your dinner counted as one kind of win; impregnating and giving birth were other types. The object of the game was to accumulate the most wins before you finally lost; in many parts of the world, it still is. (This strategy is explicitly built into video games.) Our brains developed as survival tools in the jungle game and its subgames, and even today we tend to react to many social situations as we do to games. The main differences between primitive and civilized forms? In the tropical jungle, your opponents are mostly other species; in the concrete jungle, they are mostly other humans. Among the more affluent players, the stakes are more often money and power than life and death, but in some countries, many are quick to raise the ante. In politics, one of the goals is to change the rules to favor one's own side. This makes the government into a fellow player and too often into a rival.

It would be easy to pull an Isaac Asimov and digress into the history of game theory. But even Asimov could not make it less technical nor more immediately relevant to coin collecting and investing. Instead, theorists have primarily been trying to apply the theory to such higher-stakes games as labor/management negotiations and arms talks. Game theory works better for long-run strategies than for short-term tactics; it does not tell you when to bluff or even cheat—or whether to, or why.

Nevertheless, game theory, despite its limitations, does provide a useful model for coin collecting and investing. Let's share a few basic principles from a more general but less familiar angle, one the game theorists have not yet explored in depth.

Games—including coin collecting and investing—can be played in any of three modes: ZERO SUM, ZERO DIFFERENCE, or FINITE SUM. The strategies are very different, even when the rules are the same. A single action can be a simultaneous move in more than one ongoing game; its interpretation differs with its context. The object of the same game may be different to different players; the tactics have to be, or the game would be as predictable as tick-tack-toe (where first move can force a win, second move a draw) and no more fun. It helps to know which mode your fellow players are using: are they friends or rivals?

In a *zero-sum* game, the master principle is "winner take all": your win equals your opponent's loss, and vice versa. Each player has a smaller chance at a bigger payoff than when playing in the other modes. Winner's high is generally believed to be worth its cost in previous losses, though it is not usually counted among the payoffs because theorists don't know how to measure it. Play can be fair or unfair: fair, when all players know and play by the same rules; unfair, when at least one player is misled into believing that the others are playing by the same rules, when in fact some are not. Keeping the rules vague and partly concealed works to the advantage of unfair players and to the disadvantage of the rest. The higher the stakes, the more likely some players are to mistake the game for real life and play accordingly—and the more likely that the game is rigged: "all's fair in love, war, and business." Here, winner's high becomes an explicit surrogate for killer's high. If you doubt me, listen to the way some people talk about "making a killing" in the stock market—or in commemorative coins. And was it David Merrick or Gore Vidal who came up with "It is not enough that I should succeed—others must fail"?

When the game of coin collecting and investing is played in zero-sum mode, competition is taken for granted, while too often fairness cannot be. In extreme cases ("playing hardball"), the dealer explicitly assumes that the collector or investor is hunting for bargains (cherrypicking) and/or trying to chisel down the price of any item; the collector or investor assumes that the dealer talks down coins when buying, talks up coins when selling, and overcharges whenever he thinks he can get away with it. Too often, some or all of these assumptions are correct. When they are, the dealer tends to depend on a large turnover of suckers. Ambivalence becomes a logical attitude: the collector would rather deal with someone he or she can trust to act in both their interests but nevertheless suspects that the desired item might cost too much more elsewhere—if it is available at all. The dealer's maxim then becomes "Don't knock sharp business practices—in my shoes you'd do the same thing." The collector's or investor's appropriate motto is *Caveat emptor* (Let the buyer beware). This underlies the whole controversy over grading standards.

In a *zero-difference* game, any win or loss is automatically shared: "We're all in this together." Each player has a larger chance at a smaller payoff than in zero-sum games. The classical example is hunter-gatherer groups. Here, each player's win is a share in the catch; loss would mean abandoning the hunt and going home hungry with no food for the family. The prime difficulty in zero-difference games is finding enough players to make a win possible and convincing them that the game is what it claims to be. Organizing groups such as musical ensembles or mountaineering teams is less difficult, because the objectives are well defined. The payoff mingles winner's high with the "warm rosy glow" of having accomplished something worth doing in itself or helpful to fellow players. Nonplayers are apt to think that these activities are nongames or to assume that someone is using a winning strategy of deceit by masking a zero-sum game as something else. The safest strategy is to ask, "If this proposal goes through, who wins? who loses? and who pays?"

Too rarely, coin collecting and investing are played in zero-difference mode: the hardest way to get rich. Here, the dealer passes on savings, explicitly relies on goodwill, guarantees that his merchandise is as represented, and tries to cultivate repeat trade.

Beware: one of the most common zero-sum game strategies is pretending to play in zero-difference mode. Here, the object is to deceive a fellow player into believing that his or her relationship is a rare genuine instance of cooperation. "I'm passing on these savings to you." If you make people believe that an item is a bargain, they will be more likely to buy it. Your best defense: an intact "malarkey filter." A necessary part of such a "filter" is knowing the right questions to ask: what's in it for him? how do I know that he knows what he's talking about? how do I know that his offer is honest? how do I know that the merchandise is as represented? what else do I need to find out before deciding whether to buy? Secrecy is at best a necessary evil; it always helps the dishonest more than the honest; at worst, it becomes a weapon. The collector or investor can help cut losses by comparing notes with other collectors or investors who have dealt with the same firm.

In a *finite-sum* game, any win or loss is automatically shared, but the payoffs differ with the players (e.g., buyer and seller). Strategies differ according to who defines the payoffs. A classical example: show-business groups, to win the goal of high box-office receipts, import stars at fees far above what the other players will receive; box-office receipts measure the win and the payoffs. Another game that can be played in this mode is teaching, where the payoffs include "achiever's high" (the pupil's sudden flash of insight) and "teacher's high" (in perceiving that the pupil has gotten it)—making up, in part, for inadequate salary for teacher, and lesson costs for pupil. Play is fair when all parties agree to the unequal payoffs and unfair when vital information is concealed, especially about subsequent changes in payoffs. The strategies respectively resemble those of zero-difference and zero-sum games.

More often, coin collecting and investing are played in finite-sum mode. Here the major issue is which strategies are being used and, in particular, what information is being withheld. Too often, regrettably, the tendency is to revert to the zero-sum mode. This is hardly surprising: after all, the two main character-building exercises in the United States are football and poker. Both are zero-sum games in which the stakes can become alarmingly high—in televised bowl games and Texas poker, they can become high enough to be mistaken for real life. In poker, winning strategies always include bluffing:

successful deceit is legitimized and rewarded. The poker mind-set has been applied for generations in politics and international diplomacy and more recently in coin dealing. Your only defense: if you don't know your coins, know your dealer; if you don't know enough about either, learn as much as possible before you start investing. The late Aaron Feldman's slogan still applies: "Buy the book before the coin."

In the meantime, while you are learning the ins and outs of coin collecting and investing, Scott Travers' book will help you stay in the game a little longer. Have fun.

—WALTER BREEN

Rare Coin Wealth Building

Wealth is an awe-inspiring word representing the embodiment of many people's dreams. Merely mentioning the word conjures up images of chauffeur-driven limousines, diamond necklaces, penthouse apartments, and extravagant estates. Many people want wealth, but few are really willing to take the steps necessary to gain it. Sure, if you buy a car, you are adding to your net worth, and thus, your wealth. But *real* wealth does not come from the casual, major purchase. Real wealth requires planning. Perhaps most crucial of all, real wealth requires time and patience.

Everybody has a dream. But the translation of your hopes and goals into a viable working reality requires more than living from day to day, spending all of your after-tax income on disposable goods.

You need to build wealth—assets that can ultimately be converted into income. If you have bought your house or apartment, you have taken a step in the right direction. But you need more than that.

TRADITIONAL INVESTMENTS

Part of your holdings may include stocks, bonds, commodities, or other paper assets. Traditionally, these assets have performed sporadically at best. Unless you are an expert at predicting takeovers and mergers (or have an inside source of information), you will have a difficult time making a fortune in stocks. And unless you are an expert at analyzing where interest rates are headed or predicting the stability of municipalities, bonds are not likely to be your best overall holding.

Other paper investments are just as difficult to understand. In fact,

1

you are not really expected to understand them. You merely have a piece of paper for your money, with blind faith that you are protected by the system.

To a large extent, you are protected. The Federal Deposit Insurance Corporation (FDIC) and Federal Savings & Loan Insurance Corporation (FSLIC) insure depositors for up to $100,000 per account. Those once high-yielding bank money market funds are thus protected to a limited extent (interest rates remain comparatively low as of 1990). And the Securities and Exchange Commission (SEC) has strict compliance requirements for many traditional investment areas.

The stock market's October 1987 plunge has caused many investors to reexamine their portfolio strategy. Many persons are now more comfortable with cash in liquid parking places than in traditional investments. Consequently, many financial professionals are welcoming new and dynamic financial instruments such as rare coins.

But unlike traditional investments, rare coins are generally not regulated like securities or commodities, even if they have been independently graded by a grading service, a process which might allow the coin to sell sight-unseen (this process is discussed at length in a later chapter). Many investors find this privacy aspect most attractive.

THE DIFFERENCE BETWEEN BULLION AND NUMISMATIC COINS

A number of people new to the field of hard-money assets—assets that have either intrinsic or collector value—are not fully aware of the difference between *bullion* and *numismatic* coins.

Bullion

Bullion is priced in direct proportion to the prices of precious metals. For example, if gold is $325 per troy ounce, then the cost of buying a troy ounce of gold (gold bullion) would be $325, plus an appropriate percentage commission.

Coins that are said to be worth only their bullion value are traded strictly for their intrinsic or metallic content. Coins such as the Canadian Maple Leaf are considered bullion coins and are sold at a small percentage above the going troy-ounce price of gold.

A beat-up United States dollar that no collector would even think about for his or her collection might be considered to be worth only

Fig. 1-1. 1804 Silver dollar. This rare, valuable, and sought-after coin belonged to former Mint official Dr. Henry Linderman many years ago and was later acquired by the DuPont family. It was stolen but later recovered by the American Numismatic Association. Examples like it have brought as much as $900,000. (Photo by the American Numismatic Association, courtesy *Coin World*)

Fig. 1-2. Reverse of the 1804 dollar. (Photo by the American Numismatic Association, courtesy *Coin World*)

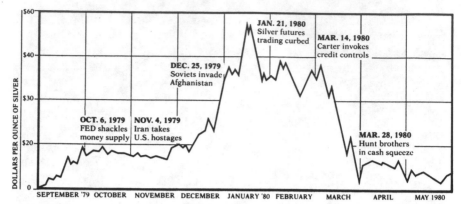

Fig. 1-3. Political events affect silver prices. The price of silver, as well as gold, is often influenced by world political events. (Graph courtesy Dennis Steinmetz)

its bullion value. If silver were priced at $6 to the troy ounce, then the bullion or "melt" value (the value of the metal if the coin were melted down) of that silver dollar would be about $4.64. Pre-1965 United States silver coins are .900 (90%) fine silver.

Bags of .900 (90%) fine United States silver coins are traded as commodities, and these bags fluctuate in value with the price of silver. The "face" value (the value you would get if you spent each coin, such as 10¢, 25¢, etc.) of each "bag" is $1,000; and the bag is not considered a complete trading unit if there is not $1,000 face value present. (Wartime nickels contain 35 percent fine silver and are also traded for their intrinsic value.)

These "junk silver coin" bags readily trade hands at a value in proportion to the price of silver bullion, although there is some allowance for a slight numismatic premium (often around 13 percent on the wholesale level). Bullion often fluctuates with world political events, as the chart that denotes silver movement in figure 1-3 indicates.

Numismatic Coins*

Rare coins, however, are not directly affected by the price of bullion. If a gold coin with one ounce of gold carries a value of $25,000, it really does not matter whether gold rises to $500 or decreases to $200 per troy ounce. That *rare* coin has its value determined by collectors who want that particular coin to complete their collections.

---

* The term "numismatic coin" is a popular one used by hard-money enthusiasts. *Numismatics* is the study of coins, paper money, and medallic art. Collectors of coins hardly ever use the term numismatic coin. "Rare coin" is the wording of choice.

Until recently (as fig. 3-6 illustrates), rare coins had an indirect correlation with the values of gold and silver. However, strict and cumbersome government regulation of bullion trading has caused bullion traders to seek an alternative to gold and silver. Many have chosen rare coins.

Gold, silver, and rare coins, as well as other tangible assets, are indicators of how wealthy people feel the economy is going to perform. In times of inflation and a deteriorating United States dollar, tangibles are in favor with investors. Conventional wisdom is that world events that shake the stability of the United States and the dollar have a tendency to cause a value rise in tangibles. However, that value rise in gold and silver may no longer follow this pattern because of the reporting requirements. *There are no requirements for reporting rare coins, and most transactions can be conducted in relative privacy.*

The value of coins is determined by the number of collectors who collect a particular series (such as Lincoln-head cents); how well that coin has been preserved (the more perfect the coin, the more demand there is for it); and how many coins of any given specimen are available (if there are two known specimens, but only one person needs it to complete a collection, that coin may not have a high value).

COLLECTING COINS BY DATE AND MINT-MARK

Some collectors collect coins by the series. This requires one example of each date and Mint-mark for a particular type of coin. The date generally represents the year the coin was released. The Mint-mark indicates the Mint at which the coin was manufactured. For example, if a coin has the letter "S" on it, this indicates it was manufactured, or "struck," at the San Francisco Mint. "CC" means Carson City. "D" indicates Denver as the place of manufacture. "O" stands for New Orleans. "P," which stands for Philadelphia, is present on some coins, but most United States coins without a Mint-mark were struck at Philadelphia. "W" indicates West Point.

AMASSING RARE COIN WEALTH: THE CONCEPT

You do not have to be a DuPont, or an Eliasberg, or a Bareford, or a Garrett—all astute rare coin wealth builders—to understand *rare coin wealth building*. And you do not need millions (or even thousands) to get started.

Many youngsters are able to get started with merely a few dollars and an eagerness to learn (read about eleven-year-old Jason Samuels in chapter 4). But to really make a fortune, you need a substantial starting sum. Or, at the very least, you need to invest smaller sums on a regular basis.

You also need a reputable dealer. Ordering coins over the telephone from a dealer whom you have never heard of is not a good method, unless you are certain the dealer is reputable; some of these dealers are slick telemarketing salesmen with little or no background in rare coins.

The amassing of rare coin wealth also requires *time, money,* and *expertise.* In order to implement your ideal rare coin strategy fully, you need a healthy dose of all three. You can implement a winning strategy with only one or two of these elements—your investment in coins just might not make you a mint, although it could still make you a good deal of money.

Time

The rare coin market moves in cycles of approximately four or five years. You need to hold on to the coins you purchase for at least three to five years to turn a solid profit. A period of ten years is ideal. While there are people who double their money in a year, *making a lot of money in a short period of time is not something that you can rely upon.*

Ideally, you should buy coins to hold for the long term with money that you do not need to survive or can afford to lose. The trick is to buy low and sell high, and that is easier said than done. You cannot always buy at the very bottom or sell at the very top, but you can try.

Money

Rare coins are a supplement to traditional modes of investment. Under no circumstance should rare coins ever be viewed as the primary vehicle. You are advised not to invest more than 25 percent of your total net worth, excluding the value of your home, in both rare coins and bullion, and no more than 15 percent in just rare coins.

You will need funds for coins. Although you may find a coin for 50¢ that you can resell for $5, that is not your goal. You want to purchase coins that you can sell later for a handsome profit. You want a coin that you can pay $1,000 for and sell in a few years for double that amount.

Investment portfolios of coins need to be diversified, just as your overall financial portfolio should be diversified. Putting all of your eggs in one basket or money in one coin is not the prudent thing to do. A starting sum of $2,500 or $5,000 is usually necessary, although you can get started with one or two investment-quality coins for *considerably less.*

Under certain circumstances, it may pay to use your numismatic holdings as collateral. Leveraging is available for rare coins—it is possible to get a loan on your present rare coin holdings to finance a new purchase (see chapter 8).

Although coins do not pay dividends or interest, you can sell off one coin at a time at regular intervals as a substitute for income, if necessary.

Coins are taxed as long-term capital gains, and like-kind exchanges are not taxable.

Expertise

The difference in price between a coin with a scratch and its counterpart with no flaws can be hundreds, or even thousands, of dollars. And if you do not know the difference, you could lose money.

The selection of rare coins requires the knowledge of a keen and expert trader experienced in the coin market's unique cyclical movement and subtle gyrations. Do not act as an expert unless you are one. If you are not an expert in matters such as grading, find someone who is.

Although there is no substitute for your own expertise, independent grading services such as the Professional Coin Grading Service (PCGS) and the Numismatic Guaranty Corporation of America (NGC) are highly reliable in their grading judgments. These organizations render opinions as to a coin's authenticity and grade and encapsulate the coin in a tamper-resistant sonically sealed plastic slab. A paper insert identifying the coin and its level of preservation is encapsulated with the coin. These coins are often traded *sight-unseen*—without the purchasing dealer looking at the coin! An increasingly greater number of dealers are participating in this slab market, and many dealerships regularly maintain and extend sight-unseen offers.

This system is the best we have, but it certainly has its drawbacks. Coin grading is performed on a continuum. There are coins that are "just-made-its" for the assigned grade, as well as "just-missed-its" from the next highest grade. Often, sight-unseen or inexperienced buyers are hit with "just-made-its" for the grade. However, what you as a buyer want are "premium quality" coins—the specimens that almost make the next grade.

There are some books and publications that can add to your level of knowledge, too. The population reports issued by PCGS and NGC are invaluable. These regularly updated reports tell exactly how many coins of each grade were graded by these services. These reports are not completely accurate, though. A number of persons are known to crack coins out of their slabs in order to resubmit them to the grading service to get a higher grade. Multiple submissions are reflected in the population reports as separate submissions, for no distinction can be made.

The Coin World Guide to U.S. Coins, Prices and Value Trends, values compiled by Keith M. Zaner, text by William T. Gibbs, edited by Beth Deisher, is issued on a yearly basis by Signet/New American Library and *Coin World.* This essential book is by far the finest, most up-to-date and helpful annual coin price guide ever produced. This absolutely vital book contains basic, as well as more advanced, information. This may look like merely the best price guide ever compiled (and it is!), but it's really much more.

Another yearly book is *A Guide Book of United States Coins,* by the late R. S. Yeoman, edited by Kenneth E. Bressett. Although this work is not as timely or comprehensive as the *Coin World* guide, in all fairness it should be stated that it does contain some useful data.

Buyers of certified coins find the *Certified Coin Dealer Newsletter* (CCDN) an important price guide. The CCDN, referred to as the "bluesheet" because of its blue ink color, reports values weekly for the coins graded by the major grading services.

Another handy information tool is the *Coin Dealer Newsletter,* a weekly price guide known as the "graysheet" because of its color. Prices are included for every major series in a "bid" and "ask" format. "Bid" indicates what dealers are willing to pay other dealers for a given coin; "ask" indicates what dealers who own a given coin are asking for it. The real wholesale value is usually somewhere in between.

Another way of getting a feel for what is going on in the market is by reading the newsletters written by real-world hard-money gurus—not numismatic experts, but people who have a keen awareness of the direction of the tangible fields.

One such recognized authority is Howard Ruff, a jack-of-all trades (and master of all) who publishes *Ruff Times* (Target, Inc., 6612 Owens Drive, Pleasanton, CA 94566–0625). Ruff offers insightful market perceptions for rare coins as well as other tangible assets. His newsletter has the largest circulation base of any in its category.

Another hard-money follower is Gary North, publisher of several brilliant and thoughtful guides—*Gary North's Rare Coin Investment Manual* and two newsletters: *Remnant Review* and *Investment Coin Review* (P.O. Box 8204, Fort Worth, TX 76112).

There are many other tangible-assets followers who are too numerous to list but who are just as noteworthy, such as Jim Dines, R. E. McMaster, Mark Skousen, and Jerome Smith.

FINANCIAL PLANNING

Financial planning is a new, bold, and innovative profession. With more and more individuals earning higher salaries and paying more taxes into an increasingly complex bureaucracy, the financial planner has assumed a role of supreme importance in American society. This financial advisor can assist in tax planning, the selection of insurance and investments, as well as the development of a total, overall financial plan tailored to meet your needs.

How Financial Planners Are Compensated and Design Plans

Financial planners are compensated by commissions, fees and commissions, or fees alone. There is much debate about which kind of planner is best. No matter which kind you decide upon, select a planner you feel comfortable with and are certain is trustworthy.

Beware of planners who have no numismatic experience but who try to sell you coins themselves without the backing of a reputable coin firm. Planners are usually qualified to determine the general suitability of rare coins for your financial portfolio but might not be qualified to select the actual coins themselves.

WALL STREET ENTERS THE COIN MARKET

"Wall Street"

Those two little words are causing big excitement in the rare coin market. After years of seeming indifference or at most benign neglect, the traditional investment community—Wall Street—began to take a much more active interest in rare coins during 1989. The implications are enormous for the coin market: Add big new money to the limited supply of truly rare coins and you have a sure-fire formula for explosive growth in prices in years to come.

Kidder, Peabody & Co. Inc., a major Wall Street brokerage house, made an impressive entry into the rare coin field early in 1989, when it formed a limited partnership fund with West Coast coin dealers Hugh J. Sconyers and Kevin Lipton. The stake: an investment of up to $40 million in rare U.S. coins.

Soon afterward came news that Shearson Lehman Hutton, the second largest Wall Street firm, was buying and selling certified coins—those that are graded and encapsulated by third-party grad-

Fig. 1-4. Independently graded coins have changed the way coins are bought and sold. The slab on the left is an NGC coin; the coin on the right has been graded by PCGS. (Photographs courtesy NGC and PCGS)

ing services—making them available potentially to 3 million Shearson customers through 11,000 brokers nationwide.

Other Wall Street firms were said to be waiting in the wings, ready to take a similar plunge. The word being heard on "The Street" was loud and clear: Rare coins can no longer be viewed as a nickel-and-dime investment.

The impact on the coin market has already been dramatic. Buoyed by news of the Kidder, Peabody fund, the market reacted at once with a buying spree. Then, when Shearson's dealings became public knowledge, activity intensified even more. Much of this activity was tied to expectations that Wall Street's involvement would continue and accelerate. But great expectations seemed realistic, given the good vibrations and far-ranging ripples that greeted Wall Street companies' first tentative toes in these new investment waters.

The Kidder, Peabody Fund

The prospectus of the Kidder, Peabody fund called for an initial investment of $5 million, but stipulated that subscriptions "in an aggregate amount of between $25 million to $40 million" were needed for the fund to achieve its goals. The initial offering period was scheduled to close on or before March 31, 1989, but units could be sold at the end of each month thereafter.

In order to be accredited as investors in the fund, buyers had to put up a minimum of $50,000. Additional subscriptions beyond that were available for $1,000 per unit. To participate, would-be subscribers had to meet stringent financial requirements: a net worth of at least $1 million, exclusive of residences and automobiles; annual income of $200,000 for each of the two previous years; and anticipated income for the current year of $200,000.

The prospectus lists KP Futures Management Corporation as general partner of the fund. This firm is an affiliate of Kidder, Peabody. Sconyers Rare Coins Inc. is listed as manager of the fund, with Hugh Sconyers being principal officer and sole shareholder of the coin firm.

According to the prospectus, the Kidder, Peabody fund is meant to be an investment of five to seven years in duration. The blueprint for the fund called for part of its resources to be governed by a "buy and hold" strategy. In other words, certain coins would be purchased with an eye to appreciation in value over time. The plan called for maintenance of a stock of other coins with which Sconyers could act in a "market-making capacity," buying and selling as market conditions warranted.

The prospectus points out that because of its strong cash position, the fund can "make large purchases without having to delay in order to raise the necessary sums and will have financial resources of a magnitude to attract numerous proposals for major transactions." This, it says, gives the fund a substantial competitive advantage.

It also notes that the manager Hugh Sconyers can use his expertise to take advantage of "grading arbitrage" opportunities. "One of the fund's major sources of potential profits," it says, "will be purchasing ungraded coins, based on the manager's expert assessment of their proper grading, in order to recognize the profits that can be derived from disposing of such coins once they have been officially graded." In other words, Sconyers expected to reap large profits by purchasing "raw," or uncertified, coins at advantageous prices and submitting them to one of the major coin-grading services for conversion into highly liquid certified coins.

The prospectus points out that historically complete collections of coins have realized higher prices than less complete or partial sets. With this in mind, it says, the acquisition and ultimate disposition of complete sets of coins is one of the fund's prime objectives.

Under the timetable outlined in the prospectus, liquidation of longer-term holdings would not begin before December 31, 1993, with a final liquidating distribution to investors no later than December 31, 1995.

As manager of the fund, Sconyers receives a monthly management fee of up to $1/4$ of 1 percent of the fund's net assets. The fee declines as the net assets increase, falling to a minimum of $1/12$ of 1 percent. In addition, the manager receives an incentive fee based on new appreciation in the value of the fund's holdings. This is calculated annually and upon redemption of units. This can range from 20 to 30 percent of the new appreciation.

The general partner (KP Futures Management) receives an administrative overhead fee of $50,000 per year regardless of the fund's profitability. It also receives $1/2$ of 1 percent of the net asset value of each unit sold, effective as of the date the unit is purchased.

Removing the Uncertainty

Limited partnership funds such as Kidder, Peabody's appeal to many investors who like rare coins' investment potential but don't have in-depth knowledge of the field. By entrusting the portfolios to experienced coin dealers, they minimize the pricing risk investors would otherwise face—in much the way that independent grading services have all but removed the grading risk.

Typically, these funds are scheduled for liquidation at the end of seven years, with proceeds being distributed at that time.

Reliable third-party grading and sight-unseen trading have played essential roles in drawing Wall Street companies to rare coins. They have done so by dissipating the confusion and controversy that formerly clouded the coin-grading process and transforming rare coins into highly liquid assets not unlike stocks and bonds.

In the process, they have given the numismatic marketplace major new infusions of money, credibility, and exposure.

There is really no set formula as to what general investment strategy will net you the most over the months and years ahead. There are many set *opinions,* however, offered by different planners. Complex formulas can be worked out with the assistance of actuarial tables in order to predict an investment plan, but the mere changing of *one* variable can set the plan on the wrong track or require you to drastically change your plan. *When you are under the guidance of a financial planner, consult with him or her on a regular basis.*

The Need to Plan for the Future

"There is a difference between amassing wealth and investing," says James E. Bandler, a New York City financial planner and wealth-building consultant. "The tax structure in America does not allow you to make money on the basis of investing." Bandler, who serves as an award-winning chairman of Howard Ruff community forums in New York, New Jersey, and Connecticut, believes that "you really can't build wealth, but you can protect it."

In a special report created for this book, Bandler prepared a financial projection and analysis for a theoretical average family of four in which husband and wife were high-income professionals. Among his conclusions were the following:

- This couple's financial plan, as well as the plans of others, should include consideration for taxes, education, retirement, and insurance.
- From 1975 through 1985, inflation averaged 8 percent. During the period 1982 through 1985, it averaged under 4 percent. This is an important factor in this family's planning, as inflation is a primary consideration of everyone's financial plan.
- College costs based on 6 percent inflation over the next ten to fifteen years bring the yearly cost up to about $40,000, from $15,000 in 1985.
- For this couple earning $225,000 per year before taxes, the total sum of $3,000,000 will be needed by the time both individuals reach retirement age in thirty years, calculating inflation at 3 percent.
- Retirement has to be planned carefully, but rare coins should constitute a conservative percentage of this couple's investment holdings.

Understanding the Coin
Market and Its Cycles

Here is $100. (Go ahead; take it!) You are going to discover how the coin market operates: why rare coins increase, decrease, or remain stable. That imaginary $100 bill will help you understand some basic principles of coin market performance.

But the first principle you need to grasp is that the $100 I have just given you is about as close as you will come to a handout in the rare coin market. There are *no* handouts and *no* freebies. In order to acquire high-quality coins, you have to pay dearly for them.

If someone were to offer you $50 for your $100 bill, you probably would not sell it. You know that you can go to a bank or a store (or a coin dealer) and get change for the $100. Similarly, do not expect to buy a coin listed in a price guide at "$125" for $50. You would not sell your $100 bill for $50, and a coin dealer will not sell his $125 coin for $50 (unless there is something wrong with it and it isn't *really* a $125 coin after all!).

The fact that I have given you the $100 with no strings attached should have nothing to do with your declining the $50 offer: the bill is worth $100, and what you paid for it is not an issue. Thus, the coin dealer who pays very little for a coin that retails for $125, but that can be sold to another dealer very easily for $100, should not be expected to sell that coin to you for a mere $50 when he can sell it elsewhere for more money.

Now you know that there is solidity to coin prices and that the coin market can be compared to other investment markets in which items are offered as commodities, such as stocks.

There might be a time when that coin offered for $125 might be

14

available to you for less money: if the value of that coin were to decline, you might be able to purchase it for less.

But if you were to leave that coin dealer and return, say, a month later, there is a chance that the coin offered to you at $125 would *increase* in value and be offered to you at a higher price, perhaps $150 or $175. Do not get mad at the dealer. It is all a matter of understanding market cycles. A close reading of this book should help you decide if you should buy that $125 coin now, wait until next month, or not buy it at all.

CYCLICAL COIN MARKET MOVEMENT

If you were to take that $100 and buy a coin with it, you could not expect to make a quick profit. For all practical purposes, every coin you purchase is priced *above* what a dealer could reasonably whole-

Fig. 2-1. Trading at a coin convention. Dealer Richard Kraft (r) discusses rare coins with a potential customer at a coin convention booth or "bourse table."

sale it for. If you were to buy coin *A* for $100, you might only be able to resell it immediately for $75. Thus, your coin would have to increase in value by 33.4 percent just for you to break even. *Therefore, coins must be viewed as a long-term investment, as virtually any short-term sale will result in a loss.*

But this example of the $100 coin is theoretical. Commissions or dealer profits are often structured so that the higher the coin is *valued,* the lower the percentage the coin is sold at over the value (and the lower the coin is *valued,* the higher the percentage the coin is sold at over the value). What this means is that a coin selling for $100 might have cost the dealer $50, and a coin selling for $10,000 might have cost the dealer $9,500.

But let us take a look at what might happen over a ten-year period if coin *A,* which has a purchase price of $100 and, for the purpose of discussion, has an immediate resale value of $75, increases at an average of 20 percent per year, compounded annually.

THEORETICAL AND REAL PERFORMANCES

THEORETICAL PERFORMANCE OF COIN *A* VALUED AT $75

(YEARLY INCREASES CALCULATED AT 20 PERCENT, COMPOUNDED ANNUALLY)

PERIOD ENDING AFTER	VALUE
First year	$ 90.00
Second year	108.00
Third year	129.60
Fourth year	155.52
Fifth year	186.62
Sixth year	223.95
Seventh year	268.74
Eighth year	322.49
Ninth year	386.98
Tenth year	464.38

It seems simple enough: if you buy a coin today with a resale value of $75, after two years you will be able to sell it for $108. But the coin market is just not that simple. You see, coins have a tendency to all increase at once and then stay dormant for an extended period. Although price performance charts and statistics may refer to percentages "compounded annually," these percentages are *averages.*

The real increases of coin *A* would more closely resemble the following chart:

REAL PERFORMANCE OF COIN *A* VALUED AT $75

(YEARLY INCREASES DESIGNED TO SIMULATE REAL MARKET ACTIVITY)

PERIOD ENDING AFTER	VALUE
First year	$ 75
Second year	75
Third year	130
Fourth year	275
Fifth year	150
Sixth year	200
Seventh year	200
Eighth year	290
Ninth year	450
Tenth year	475

The chart designed to simulate real market activity is a far more accurate indicator of coin market performance. In fact, it helps to point out why some investors become displeased after holding on to their coins for a year or two. Even when you deal with the most honest, reputable, and ethical dealers, you probably will not make money over the short term.

Some investors become restless after the first couple of years and look up the values of their coins, only to find that their coins are valued at 25 percent *below* what they paid for them. You can imagine the reaction of a seasoned common stock trader who is unfamiliar with how the coin market operates and who follows a weekly pricing guide of numismatic coins for a couple of years and sees no activity in his coin purchases!

I want to stress once again that rare coins should be viewed as a supplement to traditional modes of investment and are not designed to be the primary vehicle. You should *never* use the money that you need to eat with or survive with to purchase coins. Coin cycles can take three or four (or more) years to occur; and if you need the money during a period of illiquidity, you could be at a very serious financial disadvantage.

Some people have looked at the impressive price performance charts and undeniably spectacular performance records of some rare coins and have been talked into placing money that they need to live on into rare coins. Reputable firms do not engage in this practice. But perhaps some slick salesman who works for an unscrupulous tele-marketing firm calls and sells an unsuspecting victim on coin "in-vestment." Many of these people are duped and end up making the biggest financial mistake of their lives. Not only might there be a significant market risk, but the coin firm might not sell what it is representing. This will be discussed at length in chapter 4. *Deal with reputable dealers.*

A TYPICAL COIN CYCLE

A typical coin cycle takes about four years to occur. Here are the signs:

First Year, Phase One

Secret: *Buy high-quality coins during this phase. Stick with coins that seem depressed the most. Do not be afraid to buy coins that are still showing weekly value decreases, as long as you pay far enough below what the price guides indicate as the coin's value.*

The first year reflects a recovery from burn-out on the part of the market. There was a spectacular increase in prices that gave way to an equally spectacular downward adjustment. Values are beginning to recover from that downturn and in some areas even show some promise for healthy profits.

This is a good time to acquire coins. However, during this period of time, a number of the strong hands among collectors will not give way and sell; consequently, the coins that you would ideally like to acquire cannot be had at almost any price, for the owners of these coins are intelligent people who know that it is only a matter of time before the market strengthens.

This does not mean you cannot buy any coins during this recovery from burn-out. Some dealers might find themselves strapped for cash and in a good deal of trouble. You might, therefore, find yourself with a sweetheart deal. But if you are not careful in your selection of coins and coin dealers, you could find yourself with some highly overpriced merchandise that some disreputable dealer sticks you with to bail himself out.

Second Year, Phase Two

Secret: *Do not listen to skeptics. Buy high-quality coins with proven rarity. Stay away from peripheral areas and off-quality coins that are often promoted as the next to increase.*

Up, up, and away! The second year of a cycle is identifiable by its electrifying price performance. Coins start to increase weekly and seem to take on a momentum all their own. This momentum builds and builds, and there is talk from some people that this is merely the beginning, while other people have good memories of the previous year and want to wait it out just to be certain that coin prices did not get off to a false start.

More and more investors are getting interested in coins because of the short-term performance and equally impressive long-term history that coins have to offer.

Third Year, Phase Three

Secret: *Buy high-quality coins of proven rarity only in inactive areas that have performed well in the past or have solid collector bases and have not yet been recognized in the present boom. Selling coins for a phenomenal profit is fine; but do not sell the nonperformers, too. Just because the market is booming does not mean that absolutely everything is booming. Hold the exceptions or buy more.*

The skeptics have turned to believers! The continuing increase in coin prices has convinced even the most skeptical coin-market observer that the increases are real and that the coin market is destined for ever-higher coin values.

The general media are now paying attention to rare coin investing, and people who were previously conservative are now willing to dabble in rare coins. The sky seems like the limit. But toward the end of phase three, there is talk, nothing substantiated, about the possibility of the increases coming to a halt.

Fourth Year, Phase Four

Secret: *Do Not Sell! Repeat: Do Not Sell! The market is experiencing a downturn, and your selling to dealers might net you a ridiculously low price. Consigning coins to public auction at the first sign of market weakness is equally imprudent, for by the time your coins reach the auction block—perhaps two or three months later—the market might really be dead, along with the auction. Take advantage of the multiplicity of opportunities and buy high-quality coins.*

The market is experiencing *burn-out*. The increases were too many, too fast. The coin market is overheating. First one coin decreases; then, like a house of cards, the others seem to follow. Before you know it, the market is crashing. Investors cannot sell their coins. Dealers are going out of business or changing their names in an attempt to escape some of their obligations.

Initially, only some weakness is sensed. Many seasoned analysts still insist that this might only be a mild correction and that further dramatic increases are on the way. During this phase, the only dramatics experienced are in the area of decreases, and the increases do not materialize.

The glory days seem to be over for good. Many cannot even imagine a time when coins will be viewed as a good investment again. A large number of dealers who made a lot of money are no longer able to make a living selling coins, so they leave the field. The general media are talking about the losses. In general, things seem as if they are bad, getting worse, and will never get better. But this is the best phase during which to buy coins. Prices are low. You need guts and money, and after a few years you might well make a great deal of money.

HOW TO DETERMINE EXACTLY WHAT PART
OF THE CYCLE YOU ARE IN

The following questions are designed to help you figure out what part of the coin-market cycle you are experiencing and should assist you in deciding whether you should buy, sell, or hold. This is not a scientific survey and should not be your only indicator. However, it should give you a broad idea of how the market is doing.

The numbers next to the answer choices should be used in your scoring of the results. The scoring ranges and their corresponding coin market phases follow these twelve questions.

1. How are the prices of rare coins performing on a weekly basis according to leading price guides (such as the *Coin Dealer Newsletter*)?
   A. Increasing
   B. Remaining stable
   C. Decreasing

2. How are precious metals (primarily the prices of gold and silver bullion) performing?
   A. Increasing
   B. Lackluster
   C. Decreasing

3. How does the general prosperity of coin dealers appear?
   A. Increased prosperity
   B. Nothing out of the ordinary
   C. Much publicity about bankruptcies

4. Is rare coin investment the topic of stories in the general media?
   A. Yes
   B. No
   C. Stories about a tangibles crash abound.

5. Are the crowds at public rare coin auctions insurmountable?
   A. Yes
   B. People are there.
   C. You mean there are supposed to be people there?

6. How are the crowds at coin conventions?
   A. A lot of people are there.
   B. There are some people.
   C. Almost nobody shows up.

7. How frequently are coins being broken out of their slabs?
   A. Hardly ever. An unslabbed coin would be unsalable, no matter what was done with it. And resubmission would not be attempted, for fear of getting a lower grade.
   B. Occasionally.
   C. Coins are cracked out all of the time! AU-58s are routinely cracked out, described by auction firms as Mint State, and the subject of frantic bidding.

8. How are the circulation figures of coin publications?
   A. High and increasing
   B. Stable
   C. Decreasing

9. Are major coin dealerships returning telephone calls to *collectors?*
   A. No
   B. Sometimes
   C. Yes

10. Are the leading hard-money asset newsletters (such as Howard Ruff's *Ruff Times*) touting rare coins as exceptional investments?
    A. Yes
    B. Occasionally
    C. No

11. How is the strength of the U.S. dollar?
    A. Weak and losing ground
    B. Stable
    C. Strong and getting stronger

12. How are world politics?
    A. Crisis is the keyword.
    B. About the usual number of problems exist.
    C. The Soviets just signed a nuclear arms limitation treaty with
       the U.S., and world peace seems probable.

Scoring: Give yourself ten points for each A answer; do not add or
subtract anything for each B answer; and subtract ten points for each
C that you selected, with the exception of 12-C, for which you should
subtract twenty points.

    Phase One/-20 through 20
    Phase Two/30 through 60
    Phase Three/70 through 120
    Phase Four/-130 through -30

WHY GRADING IS THE MOST IMPORTANT FACTOR OF YOUR INVESTMENT

The primary factor that determines a coin's value is its *grade.* Almost
everything else is secondary to a coin's grade. In *The Coin Collector's
Survival Manual, Second Edition,* I state:

> Grading is the universal language which numismatists use to describe
> coins. Coins are graded on a 1–70 scale, on which 1 is the lowest and 70
> is the highest. The amount of wear and tear a coin has endured will to a
> large degree determine its grade. A grade, then, is a description, a
> numismatic shorthand for what a coin looks like.

If you know how to grade coins, or at least have an intuitive feel
for what accurate grading is or is supposed to look like, you reduce
the risk of your investment considerably. Many market analysts have
argued successfully that the numismatic market contains almost no
market risk, but a *considerable* acquisition risk.

This means that if you buy a coin that according to the person
from whom you buy it has never circulated, or passed from hand to
hand, but, in fact, that coin *has* circulated, you stand to lose money.
You will lose money not only by paying more than you should; you
will also lose by not being able to cash in on those spectacular price

increases. However, there is no great mystery to coin grading. Much of it is common sense.

The Difference between Circulated and Uncirculated

There are two basic types of grades: *circulated* and *uncirculated*. A circulated coin is one that has been spent and has lost a great deal of its detail from being worn. An uncirculated or "Mint State" coin has not passed from hand to hand and has been maintained in a pristine level of preservation. Circulated coins can never be cleaned to restore their original Mint sheen or detail; once those delicate surfaces are penetrated by wear, that coin can never be restored.

Why Grading Is Subjective

The grading of coins is subjective to a certain extent. Coins cannot be graded by computer (yet). But there is an objective element involved, and sometimes—just sometimes—beauty can be universally recognized.

Numismatists have not defined scientific standards for the grading of coins. If a coin has a scratch on one area, and another coin just like it has an identical scratch on a different area, two coin experts might give the two coins the same grade—or two different grades! This does not mean that one expert is right and the other wrong. This means that grading involves the subjective element of human opinion.

The system by which coins should be graded has been created by the American Numismatic Association (A.N.A.), the world's largest nonprofit organization for collectors of coins, paper money, and medallic art. The explanations that follow are based on the official A.N.A. grading system as outlined in *Official A.N.A. Grading Standards for United States Coins* (Western Publishing Company, Inc., Racine, WI, 1981).

A full-color grading lesson, potentially worth millions of dollars, is provided in chapter 6. However, you need to familiarize yourself with the basics so that if I say, for example, that a certain "MS-65" has increased 200 percent in a year, you will have an idea of what I am talking about.

The Difference between Proof and Business Strike

Before we define the standards, it is important to know that there are basically two different kinds of coins the standards refer to.

One kind is known as the "business strike." Business-strike coins are struck by the Mint for general circulation and for the public to spend.

The other kind of coin is known as the "Brilliant Proof." Proof coins are struck by the Mint at least two times so that the finished coin has a chromiumlike brilliance. Proof coins are sold by the Mint to collectors during their year of issue at a premium (a price above the face value of the coin). The word Proof does *not* refer to a superior condition or grade of a coin. Rather, it refers to the way the coin was minted. Proof coins are graded on the same 1–70 scale as any other coins. (There are other kinds of Proofs, too. Some Proofs are not brilliant or chromiumlike but have a well-defined grainy surface. These are called "Matte" Proofs.)

Numerical Grading Standards

Coins are often graded on both the obverse (front) and the reverse (back). The obverse grade is stated first, followed by a slash (/) and the reverse grade. Also, some dealers use intermediate grades, such as MS-68 or MS-69. Most grading services now use all grades between 60 and 70 to best describe the level of preservation.

Mint State-70
• A Mint State-70 coin is perfect.
• Not only has this coin not been circulated, but it is absolutely free from flaws.
• It is my personal opinion that a coin in this grade cannot exist. I have never seen one, and my firm has never sold one.

Mint State-67
• The MS-67 grade is elusive, but occasionally a near-perfect example does surface.
• This coin will appear almost perfect.
• Remember, Mint State coins cannot contain wear on their highest points. An unscrupulous dealer will sometimes even go so far as to call a well-worn coin that has seen circulation an MS-67.

MS-67s are usually referred to in this book as simply MS-67s. It is very difficult to figure out the prices for MS-67s. These coins are so infrequently traded that it's difficult for any pricing guide to list their values on a regular basis.

Mint State-65
This is the most frequently traded investor-quality coin. The MS-65 coin is of high enough quality to be traded frequently and rare enough to be highly desirable as a collector coin.

- The MS-65 coin has no trace of wear and has full luster, but may have light toning (the natural result of oxidation that forms on a coin over months and years).
- The marketplace often dictates that MS-65s be virtually mark-free.
- Do not think that just because a coin is bright means that it is MS-65. In fact, many intelligent numismatists *prefer* coins with toning. Toning gives a coin personality and usually does not detract from any grade.
- Although the MS-65 coin cannot have excessive marks, nicks, dents, cuts, or scratches, an MS-65 is not perfect; and there is room for very minor detractions.
- An MS-65 is generally expected to exhibit all of the detail that the Mint intended it to display. Sometimes, a coin is manufactured at the Mint with less detail than usual. This is referred to as a "weakly struck" coin. The coin is not physically worn; rather, it was manufactured with less detail than could be expected from that particular series. *Weakly struck coins will not command MS-65 prices no matter how well preserved they are.*

The existence and desirability of the MS-65 is what helps make the rare coin marketplace the bastion of liquidity that it is. MS-65 prices are amply covered in many price guides. And at a moment's notice, it is often possible to know what your coins are worth.

Unlike some of the other collectibles fields, the coin field is price-guide organized. You can pick up a price guide and know, generally, what your coins are worth. In many other fields, including the art market, you have to use auction prices-realized and guesstimates.

Mint State-64

- The MS-64 should show no trace of wear, and a cursory glance at a coin deserving of this grade would indicate that a grade of MS-65 is in order.
- Close inspection of the MS-64 reveals a detracting overall characteristic, such as the lack of full Mint bloom or too many surface marks.
- What sets the MS-64 coin apart from its MS-63 counterpart is its nearly convincing claim to MS-65.
- The marketplace has determined that if an MS-65 of a certain coin is valued at, say, $10,000, but its MS-63 counterpart is only worth $500, then the coin valued at $3,000 has to be graded MS-64.
- The MS-64 coin can be lightly fingermarked or exhibit weakness of its strike in important areas.
- The MS-64 coin is indisputably better than an MS-63 but not deserving of the MS-65 grade and, usually, the accompanying high MS-65 price.

Mint State-63
- The MS-63 should also show no trace of wear.
- MS-63s can display detracting marks that are visible to the unaided eye.
- Despite what some people say, it is my opinion that the difference between MS-63s and MS-65s (where the dollar differential can be thousands of dollars) can be taught. *There is no great mystery to coin grading. Much of it is common sense.*

Mint State-60
This is the minimum grade a coin can be assigned and still be Mint State.

- An MS-60 will often display large scratches.
- There should be no wear on the very highest points.

About* Uncirculated-55
- An AU-55 will have the very lightest trace of wear on its highest points.
- A common giveaway that a coin is not Mint State is the fact that the very highest points are lighter in color than the rest of the coin.

This is a tricky grade, and you are advised to study the photographs in chapter 6 so that you will be able to identify a coin with light wear.

About Uncirculated-50
An AU-50 has slightly more wear than its AU-55 counterpart. Again, this is a difficult grade to understand, and you are urged to study closely the color photographs in chapter 6.

Extremely Fine-45 Through About Good-3
The designations *Choice* Extremely Fine-45; *Typical* Extremely Fine-40; *Choice* Very Fine-30; *Typical* Very Fine-20; Fine-12; Very Good-8; and About Good-3 are terms that refer to coins in varying circulated degrees. Coins that have extensive wear are graded with the lower numbers, and coins with less extensive wear are assigned higher numbers.

---

* A.N.A. term for "nearly" or "almost" uncirculated.

HOW TO IDENTIFY COIN TYPES

You can learn about the grading of circulated coins by looking under the coin Type in the A.N.A. grading guide. The word "Type" is capitalized in identifying coins because it refers to a specific category of collectible coin: examples of major varieties. A 1986 Lincoln cent, for example, would be considered a "Type" coin because it is not a rare date and represents a major series (Lincoln cents, with the Lincoln Memorial on the reverse).

The appendix lists all major United States coin Types. If you do not know what I mean when I refer to, say, a Walking Liberty half-dollar, you should turn to the appendix now.

Listed below are the coins that are commonly referred to by their designers' names. The Morgan dollar, for example, does not feature someone named "Morgan" on it. Rather, it was designed by George T. Morgan.

POPULAR U.S. COINS REFERRED TO BY DESIGNER NAME

COIN TYPE	DESIGNER'S NAME	ISSUE DATES
Barber dime	Charles E. Barber	1892–1916
Barber quarter	Charles E. Barber	1892–1916
Barber half-dollar	Charles E. Barber	1892–1915
Gobrecht dollar	Christian Gobrecht	1836–39
Morgan dollar	George T. Morgan	1878–1921
Saint-Gaudens double-eagle	Augustus Saint-Gaudens	1907–33

HOW TO USE GRADE FLUCTUATION TO YOUR ADVANTAGE

Well, now you know what MS-65 generally means. You might think that it is a simple matter for this most popular investment grade to be clearly and scientifically defined. The truth is that the requirements for the grade have changed over months and years.

In general, coin grading standards have become tighter as investors, collectors, and dealers have become more numismatically sophisticated. But despite these increasingly rigid industry standards, when the coin market heats up, grading standard interpretations become loose. And when the market is falling, standards interpretations become tight. When business takes place as usual, grading standard interpretations tend to be the most objective.

The truth of the matter is that some coins (often MS-64s) that are technically very close to MS-65, but are not deserving of the grade, are bought and sold by dealers at the full MS-65 price during coin-market booms. There are so few coins available to fill demand that dealers are placed under immense pressure to deliver MS-65s to investors who are familiar with past price performance. So MS-64.9 (a grade used here only for dramatization purposes) coins realize MS-65 prices when traded in the marketplace.

You might be able to capitalize on this by buying coins before a boom that are very close to MS-65 but do not quite make the grade. Theoretically, you would be able to sell these coins during the boom at full MS-65 prices. If you do this, be certain that you are a trained expert or hire a brilliant (and honest) numismatic mind to do the buying for you. You might get stuck with overpriced MS-63s if you are not careful.

The following public auction prices-realized serve to document the grade fluctuation theory. The sale was held by Harmer, Rooke Numismatists, Ltd. at a time when interest in high-quality coins was picking up rapidly. The coins were graded accurately when the market was less heated (January 1985), but the auction was held in March 1985, when a feverish demand developed for MS-65s. What happened was that those near MS-65s realized absolutely spectacular multiples of their estimated values, and most of the coins were bought by dealers for resale.

These results are self-explanatory. The greatest interest in March 1985 was in Liberty Seated coinage. Circulated coins, no matter how rare, just were not in demand. And copper coins, such as Indian and Lincoln head cents, were on the decline. The coins whose prices-realized appear in boldface deserve your close scrutiny because they realized such spectacular multiples of their estimated prices.

SELECTED PRICES OF THE DR. WILLIAM F. MEGGERS COLLECTION OF UNITED STATES COINS, MARCH 28, 1985

COIN & GRADE	ESTIMATE	PRICE REALIZED
1877 1¢ AU-55	1,000	1,100
1908-S 1¢ MS-63	375	374
1909-S Indian 1¢ MS-60	300	275
1909-S Lincoln 1¢ MS-63 +	300	210
1909-S V.D.B. 1¢ AU-55	400	374
1873 2¢ Proof-60	1,500	1,375
1877 3¢N Proof-63 + Spotting	1,500	2,365
1878 3¢N Proof-63 + Spotting	1,100	1,320
1885 3¢N Spotted Proof	750	687

COIN & GRADE	ESTIMATE	PRICE REALIZED
1886 3¢N Dingy, Spotted Proof	400	528
1858 3¢S Proof-60 Hairlines	800	**2,530**
1869 3¢S MS-63	850	**2,970**
1794 ½ 10¢ Fine	1,000	506
1795 ½ 10¢ Fine +	1,300	880
1796 ½ 10¢ Very Fine	1,700	1,430
1797 ½ 10¢ Very Fine	1,700	1,045
1866 ½ 10¢ Proof-63	850	1,320
1877 5¢ Proof-63	1,200	2,035
1878 5¢ Proof-63	1,250	1,375
1879/8 5¢ Proof	2,500	1,320
1880 5¢ Dull Proof	750	770
1881 5¢ Proof-63	750	825
1884 5¢ Proof	500	340
1885 5¢ Proof-60 +	900	1,155
1885 5¢ Proof-65 save for spots	1,500	1,980
1886 5¢ Proof-65 save for spots	850	742
1796 10¢ Fine	1,200	1,210
1797 13 stars 10¢ Very Fine	1,600	1,815
1807 10¢ Some might see as Unc.	4,500	7,150
1863 10¢ Proof-63 Hairlines	900	**2,420**
1868 10¢ Proof-63	900	**1,980**
1869 10¢ Proof-63 Finger-ridged tone	900	**2,970**
1875 10¢ MS-63 Reverse bagmarks	500	**2,200**
1881 10¢ Proof-63 Spot over the head	750	**1,870**
1882 10¢ Proof-63 Deeply toned	750	**1,760**
1883 10¢ Proof-63 Uneven deep toning	750	**1,650**
1885 10¢ Proof-63 Blue and gold toning	750	**2,200**
1888 10¢ Proof-63 Grayish toning	750	**1,595**
1889 10¢ Proof-63 Dimpled interruption	750	**1,870**
1895 10¢ Proof-63 Peripheral obv. tone	750	**2,970**
1796 25¢ Strong Fine	3,500	3,190
1804 25¢ Good-4	550	495
1851 25¢ Fine and		
1856 25¢ Fine	75	37
1852 25¢ Choice AU	300	**1,350**
1863 25¢ MS-63	1,000	**4,400**
1869 25¢ Proof-60 +	450	**1,100**
1879 25¢ MS-63	1,000	**3,520**
1880 25¢ MS-60 +	600	**5,280**
1881 25¢ MS-60 +	700	**4,840**
1885 25¢ MS-65 Stunning blue, gold	4,000	**6,600**

COIN & GRADE	ESTIMATE	PRICE REALIZED
1886 25¢ MS-65 Minute ding at "1"	4,250	**5,500**
1887 25¢ MS-63 + Two tiny scratches	1,500	**3,960**
1888 25¢ Proof-60 + Hairlines	400	**1,155**
1836 50¢ Strong EF Prooflike	1,800	1,320
1843 50¢ AU Prooflike	150	**319**
1854 Arrows 50¢ MS-60 +	1,250	**2,530**
1874 Arrows 50¢ MS-60 +	950	**3,960**
1877 50¢ MS-60 + Light contact mark	575	**1,430**
1890 50¢ Proof-60 Hairlines, contact	600	**1,155**
1795 $1 VF-30 Draped Bust, sm. eagle	1,850	1,375
1796 $1 VF-30 Sm. date, lge. letters	1,000	880
1850 $1 EF +	1,150	770
1850-O EF	950	742
1854 $1 MS-63 + 3-4 rev. contact marks	4,500	**19,250**
1855 $1 EF	1,250	935
1879-CC $1 MS-60 +	750	**2,090**
1884-S $1 AU-55	175	**880**
1884-CC $1 MS-63	100	**550**
1893 $1 MS-63 + Lip dig and hairline	700	**1,870**
1898-S $1 MS-63 Obv. planchet defect	250	**990**

Price Performance Statistics

There is little question that rare United States coins are an exceptional investment with a superior return. But many people have wondered just how good an investment coins are. Can you reasonably expect a 200 percent increase in value per year—or merely 20 percent?

Many reputable dealers (and some not so reputable ones), eager to sell coins to investors, quote the statistical conclusions of a four-page investment policy released yearly by the stock research division of Salomon Brothers Inc., a highly respected and powerful investment banking firm (One New York Plaza, New York, NY 10004; telephone 212/747-7246). The results of this survey, often referred to in the coin field as the "Salomon Brothers Study," are released during the first week of June every year and have been issued since 1974.

As figure 3-1 indicates, according to Salomon Brothers Inc., rare coins have been the number *one* performer (at 16.6 percent compounded annually) over the twenty-year period ending June 1, 1989. A reading of the entire study reveals that over the one-year period coins ranked third, with an impressive 30.2 percent compounded annually. And over the five-year period, coins ranked fourth with 14.5 percent compounded annually. Over the ten-year period, though, coins finished second, at 12.9 percent.

The survey results are tabulated by Salomon Brothers Inc., based on valuations of coins submitted annually by Stack's, a coin dealership. The valuations are apparently based on a random sampling of United States coins. Harvey G. Stack, a principal in the dealership, indicated that his firm has been highly conscientious in its compiling of the yearly values and that at all times the value at the end of the period is used. He said that auction prices realized are the primary tool in assessing coin values for the survey.

Stack and his firm are apparently making every effort to compile the results responsibly and should be commended for performing this public service. However, it should be understood that this survey

COMPOUND ANNUAL RATES OF RETURN

	20 YEARS	RANK	10 YEARS	RANK	5 YEARS	RANK	1 YEAR	RANK
Coins	16.6	1	12.9	2	14.5	4	30.2	3
Chinese Ceramics[a]	13.3	2	8.7	6	12.2	5	40.3	2
Gold	11.5	3	2.8	10	−1.6	11	−20.5	13
Old Masters[a]	10.9	4	9.6	5	18.4	2	50.7	1
Diamonds[b]	10.4	5	8.3	7	10.7	6	15.5	5
Stocks[c]	10.3	6	17.0	1	20.1	1	24.5	4
Treasury Bills[c]	8.6	7	10.0	4	7.2	7	7.8	7
Bonds[c]	8.6	7	10.9	3	17.6	3	11.2	6
Oil	8.3	8	1.2	11	−10.7	13	3.2	11
Housing	7.6	9	5.5	9	5.1	9	6.6	8
CPI	**6.3**	**10**	**5.7**	**8**	**3.5**	**10**	**5.2**	**10**
U.S. Farmland	6.0	11	−0.5	13	−5.3	12	5.9	9
Silver	5.5	12	−4.6	14	−11.2	14	−23.2	14
Foreign Exchange	4.0	13	0.9	12	7.1	8	−13.3	12

[a] Source: Sotheby's.
[b] Source: The Diamond Registry.
[c] Stock returns assume quarterly reinvestment of dividends. Bond returns assume monthly reinvestment.
CPI Consumer Price Index.
Note: All returns are for the period ended June 1, 1989, based on latest available data.

Fig. 3-1. The Salomon Brothers Inc. Stock Research Policy report for 1989. The ten-year figure is well publicized in the coin field. (Chart courtesy Salomon Brothers Inc.)

may not be as scientific as some purport it to be, even though reasonable efforts to assure its accuracy have been taken.

Newsletter publisher Maurice Rosen made available a list of twenty coins that an authoritative source at Salomon Brothers Inc. says were the survey coins. However, this could not be either confirmed or denied by Salomon Brothers Inc. or Stack's.

If it is true that this twenty-coin list is used, there might be no Gem coins in the study, although most of the coins listed are Mint State examples.

In *The Investor's Guide to United States Coins,* by Neil S. Berman with Hans M. F. Schulman (The Coin & Currency Institute, 1986), the composition of the Salomon survey is apparently revealed. These are listed by Berman and Schulman as the survey coins:

1795 Draped Bust dollar, B.U.
1881 Trade dollar, B.U. (Proof)
1862 Liberty Seated half-dime, B.U.
1807 Draped bust dime, B.U.
1866 Liberty Seated dime, B.U.
1876 Twenty cent piece, B.U.

1873 Liberty Seated quarter, with arrows, B.U.
1886 Liberty Seated quarter, B.U.
1847 Liberty Seated dollar, B.U.
1884-S Morgan dollar, B.U.
1928 Hawaiian half-dollar, B.U.
1862 Three-cent silver piece, B.U.
1916 Standing Liberty quarter, B.U.
1815 Bust half-dollar, Unc.
1834 Bust half-dollar, B.U.
1855-O Liberty Seated half-dollar, B.U.
1921 Walking Liberty half-dollar, B.U.
1866 Shield nickel, with rays, Proof
1794 Liberty Capped right half-cent, E.F.
1873 Two-cent piece, Proof

ONE-YEAR RETURNS, 1989 vs. 1988

	1989		1988
Old Masters	50.7%	Diamonds	24.9%
Chinese Ceramics	40.3	Coins	14.0
Coins	30.2	Old Masters	13.4
Stocks	24.5	Chinese Ceramics	10.5
Diamonds	15.5	Foreign Exchange	8.6
Bonds	11.2	Bonds	6.2
Treasury Bills	7.8	Treasury Bills	6.0
Housing	6.6	**CPI**	**3.8**
U.S. Farmland	5.9	Gold	3.1
CPI	**5.2**	U.S. Farmland	3.1
Oil	3.2	Housing	1.5
Foreign Exchange	−13.3	Stocks	−4.9
Gold	−20.5	Silver	−7.4
Silver	−23.2	Oil	−9.4

Note: All returns are the period ended June 1, 1989, based on latest available data.

Fig. 3-2. Salomon compound annual rates of return. This is another chart from the Salomon report. (Chart courtesy Salomon Brothers Inc.)

It is my opinion that any number of coins fewer than several hundred would not constitute an accurate reflection of coin market performance.

Fortunately, other statistical results also confirm the exceptional performance of rare coins. Studies by *Fact* and *Money* magazines, as well as by professional numismatist David Hall, hard-money-asset expert Gary North, and others, confirm that rare United States coins are an outstanding long-term investment.

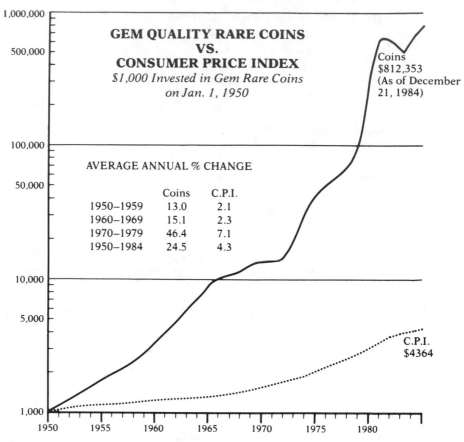

Source: 35 Year Price History, 1983 Economic Report of the President, 1984 Survey of Current Business.

Fig. 3-3. A comparison from 1950 through 1984 of MS-65 coins to the Consumer Price Index. Note the dip during 1980. The coin market has since seen much recovery. A problem with this graph, and with all indicators of price performance, is the changing of grading standards. Today's new MS-65 standards might only mean that one out of every ten coins purchased as MS-65 in 1979 would meet today's standards for MS-65. (Graph courtesy *David Hall Rare Coin Study*)

David Hall, a dealer in MS-65-quality United States coins, is the compiler of the often-quoted *Rare Coin Study*. Hall has compared "Gem" (by which he means MS-65) coins to the Consumer Price Index, stocks and bonds, three-month Treasury bills, and gold and silver. And, yes, coins come out on top, as figures 3-3, 3-4, 3-5, and 3-6 illustrate.

Hall concedes, however, that his study is not 100 percent correct and does cite some problems that make it impossible to construct a rare coin price history that is completely accurate. A major difficulty that Hall encountered was that his primary source, the *Coin Dealer*

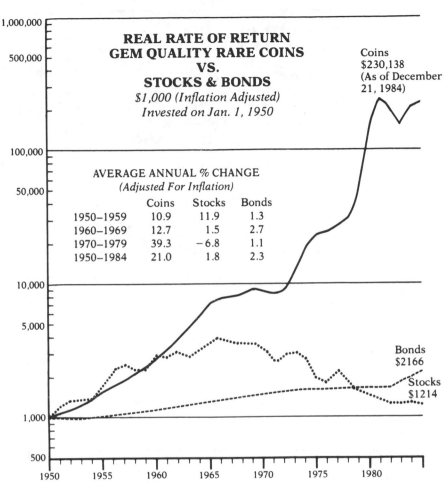

REAL RATE OF RETURN
GEM QUALITY RARE COINS
VS.
STOCKS & BONDS
$1,000 (Inflation Adjusted)
Invested on Jan. 1, 1950

Coins
$230,138
(As of December
21, 1984)

AVERAGE ANNUAL % CHANGE
(Adjusted For Inflation)

	Coins	Stocks	Bonds
1950–1959	10.9	11.9	1.3
1960–1969	12.7	1.5	2.7
1970–1979	39.3	−6.8	1.1
1950–1984	21.0	1.8	2.3

Bonds
$2166

Stocks
$1214

Source: 35 Year Price History, 1983 Economic Report of the President, 1984 Survey of Current Business.

Fig. 3-4. A comparison from 1950 through 1984 of MS-65 coins to stocks and bonds. Stocks and bonds can be measured on a uniform scale, but rare coins cannot. The *Coin Dealer Newsletter*, the primary measure of value fluctuation, cannot be used for values since 1950, since that newsletter began publication on June 14, 1963. In fact, in 1950, the grade or designation "MS-65" was not used (or even known) as a grade for regular-issue United States coins. (Graph courtesy *David Hall Rare Coin Study*)

Newsletter, did not begin publishing until 1963, though his survey begins in 1950. He used past editions of Yeoman's *A Guide Book of United States Coins* (1950–62) as the source to fill in the gap.

Coin World, the popular numismatic newspaper, has compiled a series of comprehensive price performance charts that indicate the performance of *all* United States coins, not just the Mint State examples. These have been computerized and are interpreted in the

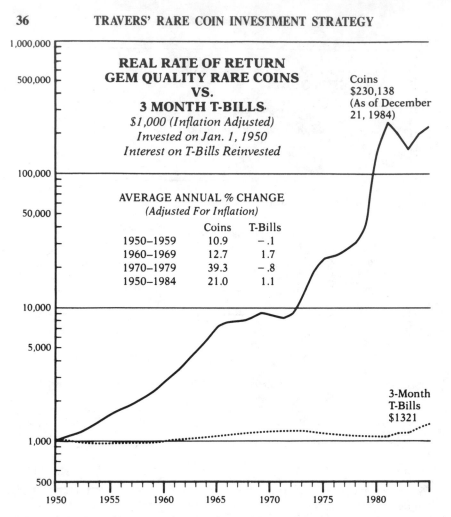

Source: 35 Year Price History, 1983 Economic Report of the President, 1984 Survey of Current Business.

Fig. 3-5. A comparison from 1950 through 1984 of MS-65 coins to three-month Treasury bills. Despite any drawbacks in the measurement of United States coin prices, coins are still recognized as top performers. These graphs should be viewed as indicators of general trends. (Graph courtesy *David Hall Rare Coin Study*)

magazine by the ingenious "Trends" editor, Keith M. Zaner. The graph in figure 3-7 is among the most accurate and reliable, if not *the* most accurate and reliable performance record available.

A GRADING RENAISSANCE

As mentioned in chapter 2, grading standard interpretations change with market conditions. As the coin market heats up, grading standard interpretations loosen. As the market cools off, interpretation of

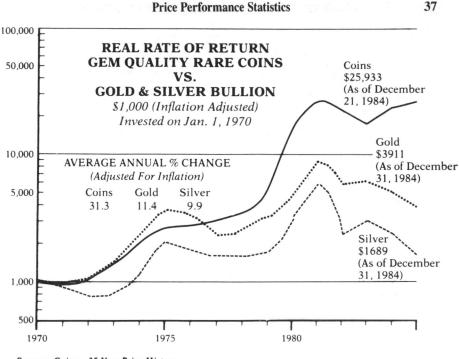

REAL RATE OF RETURN
GEM QUALITY RARE COINS
VS.
GOLD & SILVER BULLION
*$1,000 (Inflation Adjusted)
Invested on Jan. 1, 1970*

Coins
$25,933
(As of December
21, 1984)

AVERAGE ANNUAL % CHANGE
(Adjusted For Inflation)

Coins	Gold	Silver
31.3	11.4	9.9

Gold
$3911
(As of December
31, 1984)

Silver
$1689
(As of December
31, 1984)

Source: Coins—35 Year Price History.
Gold & Silver—Commodity Handbook (average price for the year—New York Commex).

Fig. 3-6. A comparison from 1970 through 1984 of MS-65 coins to gold and silver. Note the breaking away of rare coins from precious metal prices during 1984. This can be partially attributed to stringent reporting requirements for precious metals sales and none for rare coins. (Graph courtesy *David Hall Rare Coin Study*)

the standards tighten. This concept was originally introduced in 1981 by Maurice Rosen in a much-quoted article in the *Coin Dealer Newsletter Monthly Summary and Complete Series Pricing Guide.*

Michael R. Fuljenz, a former authenticator and grader for the American Numismatic Association Certification Service (ANACS), the Colorado Springs–based facility that offers its opinion as to grade and authenticity for a fee, explained the grade-fluctuation phenomenon in the April 1985 edition of *The Numismatist,* the official journal of the American Numismatic Association. Fuljenz says, in part:

> Over the past five years numerous coins have shown remarkable profits on paper but in many cases actually have decreased in value. The reason for this is partly what has been termed a grading "renaissance."
>
>   1   2   3   4   5   6   7   8
> 63 --- | --- | --- | --- | --- 65 --- | --- | --- | --- | --- 67
>
> In a sellers' market, coins 4 through 8 immediately qualify for MS-65 prices because they all are close or equal to the MS-65 grade. In a red-hot

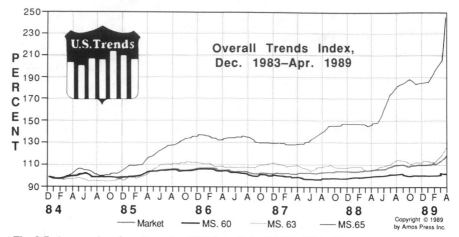

Fig. 3-7. A comparison from December 1983 through April 1989 of United States coins. According to *Coin World,* the graph is a composite of 16,576 coin values from fifty-two different series covering thirteen grades. December 1983, the base month, is assigned a percentage of 100. The index provides a market measure depicting monthly movement from this specific percentage base. The United States coin market in general is shown, as well as MS-60, MS-63, and MS-65. (This chart is a black-and-white rendition of a full-color chart created by *Coin World.*)

market, even coins 1 through 3 in some series (such as small gold coins) might trade as MS-65. As a sellers' market eventually becomes a buyers' market, customers will pay MS-65 premiums only for the better MS-65 coins; thus, only a near-MS-67 coin (number 8) would qualify for an MS-65 premium. That would leave coins 1 through 7 to trade at near MS-63 money.

This example typifies what has happened in the MS-65 market in the 1980s. Yes, MS-65 prices increased substantially on paper, but perhaps only 1 in 10 MS-65 coins from a few years ago was the number 8 coin that qualifies for that grade and price today.

It is also important to remember that in some series the best available coins traded as MS-65 during the heat of the market, so that yesterday's MS-65, in a few instances, could be today's Choice About Uncirculated or MS-60 specimen.

Maurice Rosen, writing in his *Rosen Numismatic Advisory* about the possible inaccuracy of historical price performance data, says, in part:

The most reputable and competent dealers were not immune to the power of the Grading Renaissance. In years past, they operated with the "rules" and market conditions that prevailed *at the time.* They gave fair value *at the time.* And they tended to use grading criteria for MS-65 . . . that associated itself with quotes that existed *at the time.* You see, the developing revolution of greater grading precision and pricing accuracy humbled even the best intensions of the better dealers.

Salomon Brothers Inc., too, has conceded that grading standards fluctuate. In its Stock Research Investment Policy survey, dated June 8, 1984, the firm states, in part:

> Quality grading in the numismatic market has become much stricter over the past fifteen years. Based on our survey of compound annual returns, which measures price changes in coins of a given quality, coins have ranked in the top five categories for all four periods. However, returns to individual investors who held this same basket of coins could be substantially less than those indicated, if one or more coins no longer met the stricter criteria for the quality ranking that it was originally assigned.

And David Hunt, a coauthor of the original *David Hall Rare Coin Study*, released in 1981, and a supporter of price performance statistics, who now works for Oak Tree Numismatics, admitted in a telephone interview that "the bottom level dropped away, and grading standards tightened up." Hunt meant that all MS-65s are not created equal and that the low-end MS-65s are no longer considered MS-65s.

The American Numismatic Association issued the following public statement at its mid-winter convention in February 1986:

> . . . The marketplace has tightened its interpretation in recent years and ANACS has reflected those changes. Accordingly, the ANA Grading Service, endeavoring to keep in step with current market interpretations (rather than create interpretations of its own), has in recent times graded coins more conservatively than in the past, in many instances.

> Hence, it may be the situation that a coin which was graded MS-65 by the Grading Service in 1981 or 1982, for example, may, if regraded in 1985 or 1986, merit the current interpretation of MS-63 or less. Similarly, dealers and others in the commercial sector have found that coins that they graded MS-65 several years ago may merit MS-63 or lower interpretation today.

> . . . it may be the case that the interpretation of grading standards will continue to change in the future, as indeed they have done over a long period of past years.

HOW TO CALCULATE THE MARKET PREMIUM FACTOR

Price guides are only accurate to the extent that their compilers can keep up with rapidly changing market conditions. Often, price guides have to play "catch-up." If a coin listed in the value guides at, say, $500 suddenly increases to $1,000 in a few days, the value guide will be outdated. In order to actually secure that coin, you would have to pay $500 *more* than what the price guide indicates. This higher percentage can be expressed in terms of a "market premium factor" (MPF) percentage, a concept originated by Maurice Rosen.

However, if that $500 coin suddenly loses value and is only worth $250, the price guides would also be outdated, for you could buy a coin for $250 that the price guides indicate would be worth *twice* that amount, or $500.

When that coin increases from $500 to $1,000, the MPF is 100 percent. And when that coin goes down to $250 from $500, the MPF is a *negative* 50 percent.

The MPF, whether positive or negative, can be derived from the following algebraic formula:

$$\left(\frac{X}{Y} - 1 \right) \ 100 = MPF$$

Where:
X = price required to secure coin
Y = weekly pricing-guide valuation
MPF = Market premium factor

In the case of the coin available for no less than $1,000 but with a price-guide valuation of $500:

$$\left(\frac{1,000}{500} - 1 \right) \ 100 = 100\%$$

In the case of the coin available for $250 but with a price-guide valuation of $500:

$$\left(\frac{250}{500} - 1 \right) \ 100 = -50\%$$

WHY THE BOOMS ARE FAR GREATER IN MAGNITUDE THAN THEY APPEAR

Because of the elasticity of grading standards, the price guides are not as accurate as they could be. Coins are not stocks and bonds, the prices of which are absolute at any given moment; in many respects, this makes coins a far more attractive investment medium.

During heated market periods, as has been repeatedly stressed throughout this book, near-MS-65 coins sometimes trade at MS-65 levels. So if during a boom, the MS-65 valuation of a coin increases from \$500 to \$1,000, it might actually mean that the MS-64+ is now trading at \$1,000. Assuming that the MS-64+ was available before the boom for, say, \$100, the coin referred to *actually increased by \$900, not by the \$500 indicated by the valuation guides.*

This is demonstrated and documented in chapter 2 by the listing of the auction prices-realized at the end of the chapter.

HOW TO DETERMINE ACTUAL PERFORMANCE

Of course, statistics showing how coins have performed are useful in your selection of coins. But once you have made your purchases and done some actual buying and selling, sooner or later you will want to review your investment objectively. The profit you have made is not the singular determining factor. There are many considerations, such as the time between buy and sell.

If you double or triple your money, you still might not have made that wise an investment comparatively speaking—unless you enjoyed the artistic significance of a particular coin and only bought it to study its beauty.

Business calculators, which perform functions such as exponential and logarithmic, can be a useful aid in calculating how your coins have *really* performed.

Engineer George K. Tyson, writing in the January 1984 issue of *The Numismatist,* explains with three examples, summarized below, how to calculate rare coin price performance. Tyson writes, in part:

Example 1: *Harry bought a coin five years ago for \$100. For how much would he have to sell it today to yield 12 percent profit per year?*

The general equation is:

$$\text{Value today} = \text{Value } n \text{ years ago} \times (1 + i)^n$$
$$\text{Where } n = \text{Number of years}$$
$$i = \text{Interest rate}$$

In Harry's case:

$$\text{Value today} = \$100 \times (1 + 0.12)^5$$
$$= \$100 \times (1.76) = \$176$$

If Harry sold the coin for less than \$176, he would not have received the 12 percent desired.

Example 2: *Harry has just bought a coin for $200 that he plans to keep for seven years. He desires 14 percent per year. How much money does the coin need to be sold at after the holding period in order for Harry to achieve that goal?*

The equation is basically the same:

$$\text{Value in } n \text{ years} = \text{Value today} \times (1 + i)^n$$

In Harry's case:

$$\text{Value in } n \text{ years} = \$200 \times (1.14)^7 = \$500$$

Examples one and two can actually be performed with an ordinary four-function calculator, since:

$$(1.13)^5 = 1.13 \times 1.13 \times 1.13 \times 1.13 \times 1.13$$

However, using a calculator with an exponent key (y^x) relieves the tedium.

The final problem is the most interesting and useful, but is a little more difficult, for a *log* key is essential.

Example 3: *Harry bought a coin four years ago for $150 and sold it today for $220. Was this a good investment? In other words, what effective interest rate was yielded, compounded annually?*

We use the same equation as in example 1, except in this case we solve for *i* instead of *value today*.

$$i = e^{\dfrac{\ln\left(\frac{\text{Value today}}{\text{Value } n \text{ years ago}}\right)}{n}} - 1$$

In Harry's case:

$$i = e^{\dfrac{\ln\left(\frac{220}{150}\right)}{4}} - 1$$

$$= e^{\dfrac{\ln(1.47)}{4}} - 1 = 0.10$$

Harry's investment yielded 10 percent. If he had waited another year and sold the coin for $260, the yield during the five-year period would be:

$$i = e^{\dfrac{\ln\left(\frac{260}{150}\right)}{5}} - 1 = .116$$

A yield of 11.6 percent is better. The formula is very easy once you familiarize yourself with how to operate your calculator properly; any numerical value can be substituted in the equations with ease.

The problem can also be solved with an ordinary four-function calculator. However, then it becomes a tedious trial-and-error process—especially if the number of years is large. Using example 3:

$$\$220 = \$150 \times (1 + i)^4$$

$$\frac{\$220}{\$150} = (1 + i)^4 = (1 + i) \times (1 + i) \times (1 + i) \times (1 + i)$$

You can keep guessing the value of i until the right side of the equation equals 1.47 ($^{220}/_{150}$). However, it makes sense to use a calculator that can do the thinking for you.

RECOMMENDED PRICE GUIDES

The *Coin Dealer Newsletter* and *Monthly Summary and Complete Series Pricing Guide* (weekly and monthly, respectively); P.O. Box 11099, Torrance, CA 90510, $89 per year, both publications included—recognized as the ultimate insider's informant.

Coin World "Trends"; Amos Press, Inc., P.O. Box 150, Sidney, OH 45365, $23.95 per year—a feature of the editorially jam-packed *Coin World,* the largest coin-related weekly by circulation and number of pages.

Numismatic News "Coin Market"; Krause Publications, Inc., 700 East State Street, Iola, WI 54990, $23 per year—a feature of *Numismatic News,* the concise and timely numismatic weekly.

The PCGS Population Report and *Numismatic Guaranty Corporation of America Census Report* reveal how many coins of each grade were graded by each of the services. These reports are issued regularly and are available on a subscription basis. PCGS's report (distributed by American Numismatic Exchange, 5000 Birch Street, West Tower, Suite 3000, Newport Beach, CA 92660) is issued monthly. NGC's Census (Box 1776, Parsippany, NJ 07054) is published six times a year.

PCGS Population Report, Copyright 1988

PCGS No	Date	Denom	Variety	DSIG	60	61	62	63	64	65	66	67	68	69	70
97077	1878 7TF	S$1	REV 1879	MSDM	O	O	1	6	2	O	O	O	O	O	O
7078	1878 7/8TF	S$1	STRONG	MS	16	37	95	212	104	14	O	O	O	O	O
7079	1878 7/8TF	S$1	STRONG	MSPL	3	O	12	17	15	1	O	O	O	O	O
97079	1878 7/8TF	S$1	STRONG	MSDM	1	2	1	6	1	O	O	O	O	O	O
7080	1878-CC	S$1		MS	42	93	306	625	362	77	13	1	O	O	O
7081	1878-CC	S$1		MSPL	10	14	60	87	39	9	O	O	O	O	O
97081	1878-CC	S$1		MSDM	1	5	7	8	6	4	O	O	O	O	O
7082	1878-S	S$1		MS	26	59	354	1242	1193	297	13	1	O	O	O
7083	1878-S	S$1		MSPL	2	13	48	132	81	24	O	O	O	O	O
97083	1878-S	S$1		MSDM	1	1	3	4	4	1	O	O	O	O	O
7084	1879	S$1		MS	14	18	140	382	288	42	2	O	O	O	O
7085	1879	S$1		MSPL	O	4	6	24	10	2	O	O	O	O	O
97085	1879	S$1		MSDM	2	3	5	7	3	1	O	O	O	O	O
7086	1879-CC	S$1		MS	15	15	48	81	32	6	O	O	O	O	O
7087	1879-CC	S$1		MSPL	4	8	14	13	1	O	O	O	O	O	O
97087	1879-CC	S$1		MSDM	O	O	O	2	3	O	O	O	O	O	O
7088	1879-CC	S$1	CAPPED DIE	MS	21	8	13	17	4	O	O	O	O	O	O
7089	1879-CC	S$1	CAPPED DIE	MSPL	3	1	2	6	O	O	O	O	O	O	O
7090	1879-O	S$1		MS	38	49	140	241	118	15	1	O	O	O	O
7091	1879-O	S$1		MSPL	10	8	8	12	4	O	O	O	O	O	O
97091	1879-O	S$1		MSDM	1	O	3	1	2	O	O	O	O	O	O
7092	1879-S	S$1		MS	14	61	459	2576	4610	2952	406	50	3	O	O
7093	1879-S	S$1		MSPL	7	19	119	447	678	269	32	3	O	O	O
97093	1879-S	S$1		MSDM	1	1	5	19	40	20	3	O	O	O	O
7094	1879-S	S$1	REV 1878	MS	45	57	63	61	19	2	O	O	O	O	O
7095	1879-S	S$1	REV 1878	MSPL	2	2	5	6	1	O	O	O	O	O	O
7096	1880	S$1		MS	6	23	130	459	212	29	1	O	O	O	O
7097	1880	S$1		MSPL	O	1	10	14	17	1	O	O	O	O	O
97097	1880	S$1		MSDM	O	O	2	2	8	1	O	O	O	O	O
7100	1880-CC	S$1		MS	19	56	213	571	413	111	9	3	O	O	O
7101	1880-CC	S$1		MSPL	1	10	36	49	38	7	O	O	O	O	O
97101	1880-CC	S$1		MSDM	O	1	4	5	3	O	O	O	O	O	O
7108	1880-CC	S$1	REV 1878	MS	9	11	49	80	74	17	1	O	O	O	O
7109	1880-CC	S$1	REV 1878	MSPL	1	1	3	2	O	O	O	O	O	O	O
97109	1880-CC	S$1	REV 1878	MSDM	O	1	1	2	O	O	O	O	O	O	O
7114	1880-O	S$1		MS	24	78	140	163	57	O	O	O	O	O	O
7115	1880-O	S$1		MSPL	7	6	8	10	2	O	O	O	O	O	O
97115	1880-O	S$1		MSDM	5	2	2	4	3	O	O	O	O	O	O
7118	1880-S	S$1		MS	50	139	825	4125	6982	4727	667	52	3	2	O
7119	1880-S	S$1		MSPL	8	53	260	1115	1655	850	101	8	O	O	O
97119	1880-S	S$1		MSDM	2	3	23	74	113	77	15	1	O	O	O

Fig. 3-8. A page from *PCGS Population Report*. Population reports provide credible, almost scientific data about submissions to grading services. This Morgan dollar page allows the savvy coin trader to analyze rarity. (Courtesy PCGS. Copyright PCGS 1988)

Assembling a Collection of Top Performers

Knowledge is power when you use it. If you lack the expertise, seek the knowledge of the knowledgeable—and LEARN!

—*Anthony Swiatek*

The selling of coins has become at least a two-billion-dollar industry. The collector now has to take a backseat to the investor, who often has tens of thousands of dollars to spend in one transaction. What many dealers often forget in their eagerness to please the investment market is that in the end, the primary consumer will be the collector, not the investor. Without cultivating the interests of the collector, there is really not much of a numismatic market.

But despite what anybody says, the investor is here to stay. The ideal would be to bring both collector and investor together. After all, both are buying coins. Indeed, what often happens is that a collector will develop an interest in the spectacular performance of coins by reviewing price histories. Or, better yet, a collector will turn a tidy profit on the sale of some coins from his or her collection and find the experience rather pleasant.

Or, an investor will actually look at the coins and develop an artistic feel for their beauty and cultural significance. Many people who buy coins for investment are familiar with works of art and find coins a comparable medium. These people sometimes really do become coin collectors.

If every collector would think a little bit about the investment angle and every investor would think a little bit about the collecting angle, everyone would profit. The collector/investor is a welcome breed of coin buyer.

Fig. 4-1. 1794 Silver dollar, Mint State. This is the obverse of a coin that realized a cool $121,000 during the Charmont Sale, a public auction held by Steve Ivy Numismatic Auctions, Inc. (now Heritage Numismatic Auctions, Inc.) on August 14, 1983. It is one of approximately one hundred 1794 dollars extant and is the third finest known, behind two Lord St. Oswald coins, according to Heritage. (Photo courtesy Heritage Capital Corporation)

Fig. 4-2. Reverse of the 1794 dollar. (Photo courtesy Heritage Capital Corporation)

IF YOU DON'T KNOW YOUR COINS, KNOW YOUR DEALER

People who are not familiar with rare coins are urged to become very familiar with their dealer if they intend to make purchases. There are no regulations for coin dealers, and some leave the business just as quickly as they entered it.

Although I could easily say that you should only buy coins from people who write books (and I'd narrow down your choices to a select few—myself included, of course), there are actually many expert and honest professionals who have never even written an article from whom you might profit tremendously. Below are some questions to ask. But just because a dealer does not answer something to your liking does not mean that he or she is not reputable or trustworthy.

- Are you a member of the American Numismatic Association?
- Have you ever been expelled from any numismatic organization?
- Are you an authorized dealer of PCGS or NGC?
- Do you stock books such as the redbook, the A.N.A. grading guide, and *The Coin Collector's Survival Manual?*
- Have you ever had an article published about coins?
- Have you ever provided any public service for numismatics, such as speaking at a coin club or at a convention?
- Do you go to coin conventions regularly?
- How is your recommendation track record?
- Can I make a lot of money from rare coin investment in a hurry? (If the dealer answers in the affirmative, run, don't walk!)
- If I had $100,000 to invest, what would you recommend? (Ask this question in exactly this way to the dealer or dealers you might be considering. Answers will vary and potentially prove very telling about the dealer.)
- Are you a member of the Coin and Bullion Dealer Accreditation Program (CABDAP) of the Industry Council for Tangible Assets (ICTA)?

There are many reputable dealers, and I am sure you can think of enough questions of your own to be able to determine which dealer is credible and intends to be here for the long haul and which dealer might exit professional numismatics just as quickly as he or she entered it. You are the judge. *It is your money.*

MAIL-ORDER, TELEMARKETING,
AND OTHER SOLICITATIONS

The ideal way to acquire coins is by developing a strong business relationship with the individual from whom you purchase. Many people, however, are under the false impression that rare coin wealth can be built and winners can be selected by reading through newspaper ads in general-interest publications and ordering the coins advertised. These promotions, whether perpetrated in the general press or by telephone, are often extremely overpriced. For example, you might see offered a "Set of Three Morgan Dollars for $500." The Morgan dollars might be circulated and worth a mere fraction of their advertised price.

In the January/February 1984 *Swiatek Numismatic Report*, editor/publisher Anthony Swiatek writes about these overpriced coins. He says, in part:

> The unknowledgeable are informed (via a newsletter, circulars, etc.) about how rare and how much in demand it [the coin being offered] is currently and will be in the future. It is labeled a great investment. . . . What these numismatically innocent are not aware of is the fact that the horse they have been instructed to bet on and labeled a sure winner does not belong in the horse race at all. The poor animal would have difficulty pulling a two-wheeled covered carriage in some big city park. . . . They will receive an abundant item which costs $1,000 that can be obtained from an honest dealer for $300! Can they ever regain or recoup their investment? Yes. When gold reaches $10,000 per ounce.

Stay away from the *disreputable* telemarketer. *Ask questions before you part with your money.*

If you order through the mail from *any* dealer, it is important that you are certain what grading standards he or she is using. For example, if you see a coin advertised as a "Gem B.U.," the dealer might very well be referring to an AU-50, since there is no uniform industry standard. In fact, there are as many sets of grading standards as there are coin dealers. *Be certain that your coins are guaranteed to be graded by a specific standard, such as those set forth by PCGS and NGC.*

Coin World has taken some steps toward uniformity of grading in advertising appearing in its pages. The *Coin World* policy sets a minimum numerical grading standard to which adjectives may refer when they are used to describe a coin. The *Coin World* policy appears on page 50.

ADJECTIVES	COIN WORLD MINIMUM NUMERICAL GRADE
Uncirculated	
Brilliant Uncirculated	60
Select Uncirculated	60
Choice Uncirculated	
Choice Brilliant Uncirculated	63
Gem Uncirculated	
Gem Brilliant Uncirculated	65

Coin World has instituted an advertiser checking service and notified advertisers that those who do not meet these minimum standards are subject to having their advertising privileges sus-pended or revoked.

BUY-BACK GUARANTEES

One of the latest fads in investment coins is the "buy-back" guarantee. Buyers long ago discovered a problem with the coin market: when coins are purchased for investment, the dealer from whom they were purchased often does not want to buy them back. A legitimate reason for this is that the coin is often declining in value rapidly, when the customer wants to get rid of it—but *no* dealer wants it. This also happens when coins have dropped in value and grading standards have tightened.

Nevertheless, the buy-back guarantee evolved, for better or worse. There are some real legal questions concerning the legitimacy of a straight buy-back at a percentage over the price paid. A number of people believe that this is not legal.

The most popular buy-back guarantee is the guarantee based on buy and sell prices issued by the dealer. I assure you, if the dealer were suddenly to be deluged with millions upon millions of dollars worth of sell orders, he could not possibly pay all those people the published price. (This is similar to a run on a bank.)

Independent grading services have taken tremendous pressure off the shoulders of smaller dealers who were forced by market pressures to maintain two-way markets. Coins graded and authenticated by PCGS and NGC usually have basic minimum liquid-levels. If you have a Saint-Gaudens double eagle graded by NGC as MS-65 that you want to sell and a dealer is offering $3,500 sight-unseen for that particular coin, you can sell it to him or her—no questions asked.

Coin World Policy for Advertising Uncirculated Coins

Coin World does not buy, sell nor grade numismatic items.

Coin World, through its advertising space, provides a marketplace which brings together buyers and sellers of numismatic items.

Dealers use various grading standards generally accepted in today's numismatic marketplace. Dealers are required to state in their Coin World advertisement which standard they use.

Coin World recognizes that grading coins is subjective and that the use of numbers and/or adjectives to describe the grade of a coin may need clarification.

Because of the number of generally accepted grading standards in use today, Coin World has adopted minimum standards for grading terms used in Coin World advertisements for Uncirculated coins in order that buyer and seller can better communicate.

* Uncirculated, Brilliant Uncirculated or Select Uncirculated must be a minimum of Mint State 60.
* Choice Uncirculated or Choice Brilliant Uncirculated must be a minimum of Mint State 63.
* Gem Uncirculated or Gem Brilliant Uncirculated must be a minimum of Mint State 65.
* Superb Gem Brilliant Uncirculated or Superb Brilliant Uncirculated must be a minimum of Mint State 67.
* Split grades such as MS-63/65 or MS-60/63 must fall back into the lowest adjective level. MS-63/65 may be described as Choice Brilliant Uncirculated or Choice Uncirculated. The split grade MS-60/65 or MS-60/63 may be explained as Uncirculated, Brilliant Uncirculated or Select Uncirculated.

Coin World reserves the right to monitor the merchandise offered by advertisers through the Coin World Customer Checking Service. Orders may be placed at any time at Coin World's discretion to verify that the coins are as advertised.

Any advertiser placing an advertisement in Coin World agrees to adhere to these minimum standards. Advertisers found in violation may have their advertising privileges suspended or revoked.

These standards will be effective as of the July 3, 1985, issue of Coin World.

Coin World

THE WEEKLY NEWSPAPER OF THE ENTIRE NUMISMATIC FIELD

Phone 513-498-0800
911 Vandemark Road, P.O. Box 150, Sidney, Ohio 45367

Fig. 4-3. *Coin World* policy for uncirculated coins.

50

The dealer can't say that he or she can't use it; and the dealer can't put you off until next year or even next week. If you want to sell that coin, it's sold!

Although this system is superb, you still should be certain that the coin stands on its own merits out of the holder.

If you buy accurately graded and fairly priced coins from a reputable dealer, you won't need a buy-back guarantee, for the coins will stand on their own merits. If you buy coins with a buy-back from a disreputable dealer, he or she might well find some reason not to honor the guarantee (or might not be around by the time you try to get it honored). *Do not buy coins with complete confidence from a dealer just because he or she offers a buy-back guarantee.*

GRADING: THE PROBLEM OF SUBJECTIVITY

An independent and impartial coin-grading service, which offers grades that are accurate beyond a reasonable doubt and constitutes a refined third-party opinion, has been the desire of many involved in numismatics. PCGS and NGC are these grading services. ANACS has had problems.

Grading is a subjective process, and some experts disagree with some of the grades of coins assigned by ANACS. Further, rapid turnover of personnel, tightening and loosening of standards, and inexperience cause inconsistencies.

I conducted an interview with Michael R. Fuljenz, a former ANACS authenticator/grader, in March 1985 for *COINage* magazine, the world's largest-circulation coin publication (highly recommended! $18 per year; Miller Magazines, Inc., 2660 East Main Street, Ventura, CA 93003). Fuljenz said that on a 1982 visit before he worked at ANACS, he saw staffers engage in fundamental breaches of numismatic etiquette, such as "removing a small piece of lint from a $5,000 Proof Barber coin with a brush so it would photograph better" and "examining multithousand-dollar coins on a wooden table with no protective padding underneath."

Fuljenz also revealed that one staff member would examine submitted coins "in the palm of his hand and not by holding it on the edge." (Handling of this kind can put wear on a coin in as little as an hour and diminish its value by thousands of dollars.)

A probe of ANACS, the results of which were revealed in early 1985, showed a number of problem areas, many of which have been corrected.

Les Simone, writing in the June/July 1984 *Report on ANACS Coins,* says, in part:

> ANACS has become a card game with different wild cards. No one has informed the players as to which cards were wild. Just when standards seem to be settling down, new personnel join the staff, and then [the standards are] off and running again. . . . At this very moment, the credibility of ANACS is walking a tightrope. . . . It is wrong for ANACS graders to be in the coin business. For an A.N.A. grader to have his own coins graded leaves open a doubt that special favors are being done. . . . I was told that graders do not grade their own material, but all their colleagues do. They are all friends, and they know when a fellow grader's coins are coming through. . . . A.N.A. graders should not be in the coin market, period. This means that they must also not call up collectors and dealers both before and after their coins are graded and offer to buy [those coins] for whatever purpose. . . . There are lots of enemies of ANACS. . . . As long as loopholes and special favors exist, the enemies of ANACS will have fuel for their fire.

Again, many of the improprieties that Simone comments upon have been eliminated. *Buy the coin, not the certificate or slab.*

HOW TO DIVERSIFY YOUR HOLDINGS

Coins portfolios, like financial portfolios, should be diversified, no matter how large or small the portfolio is. Every portfolio should contain approximately the following mix, unless an individual wants to assemble an entire series, such as a complete set of Wheatstalk reverse Lincoln cents (1909–1958).

5 Percent, COPPER COINS
Secret: Investors have generally steered clear of copper coins because of the vulnerability of coppers to the environment: they deteriorate quickly. Many dealers are not able to carry copper coins to Florida shows because of the high moisture levels. Stick with well-struck MS-65 or better Flying Eagle cents (copper-nickel) and spot-free Indian head cents.

15 Percent, NICKEL COINS
Secret: Nickel coins contain 75 percent copper but still do not have the stigma attached to them that copper coins do. Nickel coins are turned to as soon as gold and silver coins reach levels that are not affordable to the average buyer. Stick with high-quality (MS-65) nickel Type coins such as Shield and Liberty.

40 Percent, SILVER COINS

Secret: Beware of artificial toning. Carefully study the chapter on grading (6) before buying any silver coins. There are often great differences in price; learn common-sense grading. Check carefully for wear on the very highest points, especially on the knees and breasts of Liberty Seated coinage. If you buy silver coins during booms, pay particularly careful attention to the grading. Standards fluctuate more with silver coins than with any other metal type.

20 Percent, GOLD COINS

Secret: Check for signs of circulation, and do not let the luster mislead you. Gold retains its original Mint luster almost indefinitely.

15 Percent, COMMEMORATIVE COINS

Secret: Beware of "Proofs" that are business strikes, and always look beneath the toning—even if it is original—to see if there are major detractions.

5 Percent, PATTERN COINS

Secret: Pattern coins are coins that were never made for general circulation—designs made in limited numbers by the Mint to see what the coin would look like. Stick with the rarest and the most common. The rarest are in demand by connoisseurs; the most common can be promoted to make prices appear to be higher. There has been little price movement in this series over the past few years, but the potential for advance is great.

THE PERENNIAL WINNERS

United States Coins

The following twenty coins represent, in my opinion, the blue-chip perennial winners. The Liberty Seated Types are the varieties without the motto. Consult your numismatic advisor for up-to-the-minute values. Buy certified coins when possible.

- All *rare* U.S. coins grading MS-66 or better (certified only)
- All *rare* U.S. coins grading Proof-66 or better (certified only)
- Indian head cent, absolutely spot-free Proof-65 or better
- 1909 V.D.B. cent, MS-67 or better
- Three-cent nickel, Proof-65 or better
- Shield nickel, Proof-65 or better

- 1883 without cents Liberty head nickel, MS-67 or better
- Liberty head nickel, Proof-65 or better
- Jefferson wartime nickel, cameo frosted Proof-65 or better
- Liberty Seated dime, Proof-64
- Barber dime, Proof-64
- Mercury dime, Proof-65 or better
- Liberty Seated quarter, Proof-64 or better
- Barber quarter, MS-65 or better
- Liberty Seated half-dollar, MS-64 or better
- Barber half-dollar, Proof-65 or better
- Liberty Seated dollar, Proof-65 or better
- Common date Morgan dollar, MS-65 or better
- Liberty head double-eagle, MS-64 or better
- Saint-Gaudens double-eagle, MS-64 or better

United States Gold and Silver Commemorative Coins

The following six coins were selected in consultation and by mutual agreement with Anthony Swiatek, coauthor with Walter Breen of *The Encyclopedia of United States Silver and Gold Commemorative Coins.*

- 1922 Grant with star, MS-60 through MS-65
- 1946 Iowa Centennial, MS-67 or better
- Oregon Trail—all issues, MS-65 or better
- 1925 Fort Vancouver centennial, MS-63 through MS-65
- 1936 Norfolk Bicentennial, MS-65 or better
- 1904 and 1905 Lewis and Clark dollar, MS-63 through MS-65

YOUNG PEOPLE AS COLLECTORS AND INVESTORS

Coin collectors and investors need not be advanced in age or income. The opportunities for young people in numismatics are endless. Interested persons under the age of eighteen are invited to write to Florence M. Schook, former president of the American Numismatic Association and former chairperson of the A.N.A.'s young numismatist (YN) program (P.O. Box 2366, Livonia, MI 48154). Mrs. Schook will add each new name to the proper young numismatist mailing list used to invite YNs to free educational seminars and lunches. The programs are subsidized by participating organizations and coin dealers. Scholarships to numismatic summer seminars at Colorado College are also offered.

How Eleven-Year-Old Jason Samuels Invested

As an eleven-year-old elementary school student, Jason Samuels was already a well-known coin trader at major conventions throughout the country. He didn't trade in coins with huge price tags, but he made some stunning profits, percentage-wise, that would make some who are a multiple of his age envious.

"You have to act serious about it and let the seller think you know something about coins and have money to spend," young Samuels opined. "Otherwise, they'll take advantage of you or not want to even show you coins."

Jason's father, Lawrence Samuels, an executive with the ABC television network, accompanies his son—now a teenager—to conventions and has the opportunity to observe Jason's strategies first-hand. "Some of these dealers see that Jason has a graysheet, and they shiver behind the table because they are thinking that here's a guy that knows something," the elder Samuels pointed out.

Jason started collecting at the age of six, after his love of numbers and reading (he already knows that he wants "at least one degree in mathematical science") proved to be a good foundation for the acquisition of coins. At the age of seven, he decided he really liked collecting. He even bought himself a 1931-S Lincoln cent for $2.50, which today he values at $50.00. In that case, Jason knew more than the dealer, for he bought it as a 1931 "D," which would have been valued at the lower price.

He started with a modest allowance ("under $10 per week," according to his mother, Phylis, a free-lance artist). But Jason bought coins right. He sought the advice of experts, and he made good decisions on his own.

Jason Samuels evaluated his collection especially for this book, and reports that he has never lost one cent on coin purchases and, in fact, has made a remarkable profit on every coin.

Did Lawrence Samuels teach his son anything about coin trading? "I'm nothing but a second-class, meager assistant numismatist," the elder Samuels jested.

THE PRESERVATION OF YOUR COINS

Coins need to be preserved in an airtight environment, free from airborne contaminants. A consistent temperature should be maintained, and the humidity should be low. Ask your dealer to *neutralize* the coin before you take possession of it. This process consists of a quick dip of the coin in trichlorotrifluoroethane. Remember, this is not a cleaning of the coin. The only elements being removed from the coin are surface dust and other lightly held, potentially dangerous pollutants. Watch slabbed coins for deterioration.

Coins should not be stored in polyvinylchloride holders. These holders are soft. They should be stored in brittle holders, such as those marketed under the brand names of Capital (Plexiglas), Kointain (triacetate), or Saflip (polyethylene terepthalate). There is a test to determine whether or not your holder is made of the potentially harmful PVC. Touch a flame-heated copper wire to the holder. The plastic should melt, and if the flame is green during the melting process, PVC is present. (For further information on coin storage, see *The Coin Collector's Survival Manual.*)

A safe-deposit box used to store coins should have a vapor phase inhibitor placed in it. This changes the molecular composition of the air so that the coins will not deteriorate. A popular corrosion inhibitor, called Metal SAFE®, is displayed in figure 4-4.

Fig. 4-4. Metal SAFE corrosion inhibitor. This product is purported to help coins remain in their original level of preservation. (Photo courtesy E & T Kointainer Company, P.O. Box 103, Sidney, OH 45365)

The High-Quality-Only Syndrome

1887-S *Morgan dollar* MINT STATE (68) Prooflike. An astounding specimen with no marks of consequence upon its immaculate, reflective surfaces. Light golden toning. 100 percent fully struck. Record potential for this vastly underrated issue. On a basis to the total mint state population of the same date, this is one of the rarest of all Morgan issues.

—*Auction coin description by*
Heritage Numismatic Auctions, Inc.

The great search for that elusive quality—perfection—occurs in every area of human endeavor. The search for perfection is taught to us in school, at work, and in society. The "A" student is rewarded and held up as an outstanding example. In the workplace, the worker with the superior performance reviews gets the raise and the promotion. And in society, the search for the perfect mate or the "ideal" relationship has become legend. The cinema gave us the movie *10*, in which Bo Derek played the perfect-looking woman—a movie that either heightens our awareness of the search for the flawless or points out how ridiculous our society has become in the search, depending on your point of view.

Advances in modern technology have placed perfection at a premium. Modern computer data bases and word-processing programs have given us perfectly sorted mailing lists and automatic spelling checkers, thus making mistakes in communications virtually nonexistent. At least in the materialistic world, our society has evolved into a quality-conscious one.

In the *very* materialistic world of rare coins, the awareness of quality is supreme. The investor and the profit-minded collector are bombarded with books and periodicals urging the coin consumer to buy only the highest quality. Even many solid collectors are now content only with filling gaps in their collections with MS-65s or better. With the exception of a few contrarian newsletter writers and a handful of journalists, the MS-65 is the coin recommended for purchase. Conventional wisdom in the rare coin field is to buy the highest quality.

In fact, during the great coin boom of 1979 to 1980, buyers wanted only the best. As I have discussed in detail, many of those coins decreased in value dramatically. But many coins have recovered in price, and the quest for the best is back as a market attitude. So Ed Reiter's award-winning December 1979 article in *COINage* magazine is just as applicable now as it was then (and will probably be just as applicable in the future). In "The Search for the Perfect Coin," Reiter states, in part:

> Few would dispute that it's wise to invest in the best. There's growing concern among thoughtful hobby observers, though, that things may be getting out of hand—that the quest may have become a not-so-magnificent obsession. . . . Some of those who criticize the perfectionists express hope that the pendulum may swing the other way—toward coins that are less than perfect, and possibly even less than uncirculated, too. . . . Yet, prices for the super-coins have risen so fast and so far that the rest of the market seems, by comparison, to have virtually been standing still. And as would-be buyers find the limited supply diminishing even further, some observers predict that the demand will—and should—be channeled into second-level pieces. . . . Jimmy Carter once posed the question, "Why not the best?" As they study the market today, would-be coin buyers might well ask themselves, "Why?"

High-quality coins are touted as outstanding investments by dealers such as David Hall. In *David Hall's Secret to Profiting in Quality Coins,* a ten-page booklet, Hall emphasizes: "The biggest mistake a rare coin investor can make is to buy less than Gem quality coins. For maximum profit potential, your portfolio should consist of Gem quality coins exclusively. For the rare coin investor, quality is everything!"

David Hall's comment deserves your serious consideration, because many people in the hard-money-asset community listen to Hall. This recommendation, combined with others like it made by hard-money-asset promoters, is a contributing factor in causing "Gem" (by which Hall means MS-65) quality coins to increase. High-quality coins really have proven to be an outstanding investment. *But there are exceptions, and MS-65 might not be the best investment selection all of the time, as I have noted in previous chapters.*

It is interesting to note, however, that during market upturns, accurately graded high-grade circulated material (coins that grade About Uncirculated-55) are often unobtainable, for much of that material is sold as Mint State by certain dealers who are under intense market pressure to sell Mint State coins at competitive prices. So even if you wanted coins graded AU-55 instead of MS-65, you might not be able to find them.

MS-65 COINS AND THE MORAL DILEMMA

MS-65 coins have increased dramatically in value. Very few people will dispute this. And if you want to use historical track records as an indicator of performance to guide your investment decisions, then you should buy MS-65s. As a market analyst and numismatic advisor, my advice to you is to stick with the best. No matter how many people say that MS-65s are overpriced or will not continue to increase in price, I believe that they *will* continue to increase. They will always be attractive as investments and, therefore, most easily promoted as an investment item. Few will argue with this "buy-the-best" advice.

However, there is a moral dilemma involved in jumping on the "buy MS-65" bandwagon. From a moral point of view, I feel that there is no real justification for an MS-63 coin with a few noticeable nicks and blemishes to be priced at, say, $100, when its MS-65 counterpart is valued at, perhaps, over $1,000. I would like to personally tell those people who are buying MS-65s to buy lower grades instead because there is no real rationale behind so great a price difference. I would like to change people's behavior as a whole. If I were to try to change people's buying habits, I might be heard, but people would probably still want only to "buy the best."

There is no reason to believe that MS-65s will not continue to be in great demand. In fact, there is every reason to believe that they will always continue to be in demand. MS-63s don't always increase in value at a frantic pace, and the same goes for circulated coins. Although promoters of MS-63 and lower-grade coins have logic on their side, those individuals who recommend that the highest quality be purchased have past performance (and a heck of a lot of investors who have and will only continue to purchase MS-65s) on their side. Nevertheless, MS-63 should not be written off. Many MS-63s have performed impressively.

No matter how many dealers insist that MS-63s will be the next craze and that when investors leave the marketplace the emphasis will shift from MS-65s, the highest quality—the elusive MS-65s—still increase. Anything is possible, but there have not been upward adjustments of MS-63s anywhere close to the upward adjustments of the MS-65s. Furthermore, investors do not leave the marketplace. They continue to buy during both downturns and upturns. The investor is here to stay. The investor has invested *billions* of dollars in coins and, for the most part, plans on holding them for the long term.

Q. David Bowers, author of numerous books on numismatics and a former American Numismatic Association president, addressed this moral dilemma in a *Numismatic News* interview with Paul M. Green, the renowned Wisconsin numismatic journalist. He says, in part:

> Investors have been conditioned to believe that MS-65 is the only way to go. The result is that MS-65 is in demand by tens of thousands of coin buyers who are not numismatists. Thus, you have a two-tier market. Numismatists are sitting on the sidelines and are in many instances buying MS-60, MS-63 and other coins which have not shared in the price boom and which by comparison seem to be more reasonably priced. This seems to be an intelligent thing to do I might add. If investors keep buying coins, then MS-65 pieces will undoubtedly continue to go up in value. . . . By comparison, MS-60 and MS-63 coins appear to be bargains. This will probably mean one of two things: Either MS-60 and MS-63 coins will increase in value in order to narrow the gap, or MS-65 coins will decrease in value (particularly if investors leave the marketplace).

THE ALLURE OF MS-64

Coins that are circulated and considered relatively common are not considered great for investment purposes. Less-than-65 quality coins are often considered and sometimes shunned as investments. The thought of investing in a miserably scratched MS-60 or MS-63 with some obvious detractions might also come to mind. But few people, until recently, have seriously considered the potential of coins that are arguably MS-65s: borderline MS-65 or *MS-64* coins.

Many coins that were traded among dealers as legitimate MS-65s in 1980 are today considered to fall just short of the mark because of the tightening of grading standards. The marketplace has categorized these coins as MS-64s. Many MS-64s of today were yesterday's legitimate MS-65s.

Although these coins meet the textbook definition of MS-65 as outlined in *Official A.N.A. Grading Standards for United States*

Coins, they do not meet the grade where it counts the most—in the marketplace. The American Numismatic Association Certification Service has tightened its grading standard interpretations, so that if any of these MS-64s were submitted, they would *not* receive the 65 designation.

The high-end MS-64s may be subject to a fluctuating grading standard interpretation in the event of a wildly booming coin market. Depending on the circumstances, these coins may be traded in the marketplace as full MS-65s. As such, MS-64s, many of which are former MS-65s, have great potential.

MS-64s that make the best investments are the arguable MS-65s: high 64s, which upon first glance would appear to satisfy even today's rigid MS-65 standard, but upon closer inspection would appear not to qualify for MS-65. There is a wide range of prices, with some price guides increasingly recognizing the MS-64 grade in more and more coin types. Avoid buying MS-64s that are priced only slightly below their marketplace MS-65 counterparts.

The direction today is for precision grading to overtake the coin industry. The dollar amounts commanded for the Mint State grades for additional numbers, such as 64, are just too great not to gain increasing recognition and approval. In fact, leading grading services grade Mint State coins using every intermediate grade, including MS-61 and MS-62!

THE IMPRESSIVE PERFORMANCE OF HIGH-QUALITY COINS

You cannot deny the spectacular performance of high-quality rare coins. Perhaps success attracts success. But high-grade rare coins have performed well. And it is the historical record, combined with the fact that almost every dealer you can imagine has been using his or her clout to promote rare coins as an investment, that has caused such a great influx of investor dollars into this industry.

But to make money you need strictly graded coins that are fairly priced for the time period. As I have explained in chapter 2, in order for you to realize the spectacular investment percentages so frequently discussed in the numismatic press, coin buyers (or at least one buyer) have to believe that your coin is of that grade when you are trying to sell it. If you bought a coin in 1979 as a Mint State-67, and were able to sell it in 1983 or 1986 as only a Mint State-63, you will now realize the importance of strict grading. At the very least, you will realize that coin grades fluctuate with the market and that all the performance studies in the world showing, for instance, that MS-65 coins increase 20.4 percent per year compounded annually are meaningless if you can only sell the coins you bought as MS-65s at an MS-63 price.

In the chart beginning on page 66, I have used the *Coin Dealer Newsletter* (CDN) to show the *real* performance of MS-65 coins as compared to About Uncirculated coins during the periods 1979 through 1980 and 1984 through 1985. Accurate coin-market performance figures can only be obtained by using statistics from a publication dating from just after the beginning of a boom (to show what you would pay for a particular coin) and just before the end of a boom (to show what you would sell a coin for). An accurate performance review could be derived from either the boom period 1979 to 1980 or 1984 to 1985, but the figures comparing 1979 to 1984 would be meaningless, because the two markets viewed coins differently.

Even though the same MS-65 label was used in 1979 and 1984, the same quality of coin was not being referred to. Grading standards have tightened throughout the industry for a multitude of reasons, and the 1979 MS-65 might not measure up to today's stricter standards and, in fact, might only be considered an MS-63.

The following poetic parody from the *Rosen Numismatic Advisory* points out the tightening of grading standards:

Mirror, mirror on the wall,
"Wonder-coins" are the best of all.
At least that's what my dealer said,
As did the advisory pulp I read.
"Pay triple, quadruple, ten times bid;
They're going to the moon," so buy I did.
That lunar trip they didn't take after all,
As I went to sell my coins last fall.

Horror of horrors, a fate I hadn't sought,
Befell as my wonder-coins proved nought.
The 67s which once bedazzled my portfolio,
Had sunk to prices so disastrously low.
Besides being now called MS-63,
Their premiums disappeared it was told to me.

Is there a lesson to be gained from my woe?
Indeed there is if you value your dough:
Leave wonder-coins to the pros!

—*Anonymous investor, 1983*

THE RUSH TO WONDER COINS

Maurice Rosen, writing in his June 1988 *Rosen Numismatic Advisory,* states the following, slightly abridged (these coins increased by more than 100 percent in some cases just a few weeks after the release of this report):

NGC and PCGS. These "slab" grading services have fostered confidence never before seen in the rare coin marketplace. It has touched not only collectors and investors, but dealers as well. The fear of overpaying for coins has been greatly reduced. The fear of buying overgraded coins has been largely eliminated. As with any market, increased confidence produces greater participation. This is the key factor to propel prices to new heights.

Population Reports. These regularly issued reports by NGC and by PCGS, whereby they each publish a running tally by grade of all coins they have certified, gives us a documentation of rarity the likes of which we've never before had. In print you can see how rare a particular coin is (at least for those coins graded by NGC or PCGS). Dealer claims which tended to overstate rarity were flagrant in the past. One dealer's "rare" coin was another's "common" one. One dealer's Gem BU may have been another's AU! Any researcher worth his salt should have been displeased with the level of data that previously existed. What we now have are reasonably accurate data (improving with time) that go a long way to not only support and justify today's values for the Super Grades but allow their prices to soar amid the enthusiasm and emotion of a rip-roaring bull market.

Bull Market Fever. Picture the Great Bull Market of 1976–1980. Many dealers made fortunes. They bled the trend to the end! Profits from bullion sales and trading were plowed into rare coins. Dealers who previously only knew how to operate a coin counting machine were brashly jumping head first into numismatics buying with reckless abandon at auctions and shows. It all seems so careless to us now, of course, but such activity and attitude often characterize a heated market—whether they be tulip bulbs, land speculation, stocks, or coins. That's the nature of a market top.

It's a safe bet that high emotions will mark the late phase of the coin market's next bull market. What greater ego satisfier can there be but transactions in Super Graded coins at sensational prices? Buying calmly, sensibly, and selectively now can reward you in *multiples* when most others have lost their senses.

Quality Sells. The next bull market will likely involve a somewhat changed composition of investors and speculators than what we had in the 1970s and early 1980s. Today's prosperous, up-scale people appreciate and demand quality. The thought of shelling out big bucks for Porsches, Mercedeses, fancy watches, designer clothes, luxurious cruises, even specialty ice creams, is indicative of a "zest for the best." Thus, the appeal of Super Graded coins falls on very receptive and complying ears. To spend $4,000 for a coin graded 67, versus $400 for the same issue in 64, is no obstacle to many people.

The next bull market is likely to draw many of these big spenders. The baby boomers are now entering their 40s—a time when careers are set, when wealth accumulation is strong, and when an appreciation for the finer things in life begins to impact spending habits.

In contrast, many buyers of the 1970s were hard-money people. They believed heavily in bullion and were very conservative individuals. Coins grading 60, 60+, even 63 were largely palatable to them. Accordingly, things like BU rolls of silver dollars, $20 gold pieces and AU or Unc. type sets of U.S. gold coins were successfully promoted to them. Convincing them of the merits of buying an MS-65 Barber dime for $1,000 was a chore when they were groomed to buy 20-coin rolls of Morgan dollars for the same $1,000.

To be sure, some bought rare coins in "high" grades. But, many did not. They stayed with the assumed safety of their "bulk" acquisitions (such as BU $1 rolls, now at their lowest price levels in nearly a decade!). My point is that the general hesitancy to pay up for top quality in the 1970s will not exist to the same degree in the 1990s.

Institutional Participation. Here's the big wild card. By institutions I mean stock brokerage firms, big money managers, pension and profit sharing plans, private partnerships, perhaps closed-end funds. Much of institutional money is performance driven. Should inflation concerns mount, should gold and silver prices run, should paper investments lose their luster, you'd better believe that rare coins will be much higher on the new products agenda of these firms than they are today. In fact, some farsighted firms are already quietly engaging in due diligence studies. After one or two embrace coins, a pack rat mentality may ensue. But what will they buy?

You have to believe that they will be guided by the finest hired minds in the coin business. Moreover, institutions are used to buying quality; that was the proper game during the stock market boom of 1982–87. The Nifty Fifty of the 1960s stock market might well become the Super Graded coins of the 1990s!

Recall my statements of the highly leveraged nature of the rare coin market. It's one thing for highly concentrated money flows to zero in on $20 Saints. It's another thing for them to be advised to load up on coins grading no less than 65!

Roll Over Rembrandt. You've read about the startling record prices of paintings and other works of art: $13–$39–$54 million for van Goghs, $9 million for a diamond. One night last month at a Sotheby's art auction in New York, bidders spent close to an amazing

$100 million in less than 2 hours! What's more, the average price for a piece of art was $1.75 million! "But just as remarkable as the prices was the crowd's reaction to them. While bidders used to buzz audibly when a work soared over $3 million, this time they stayed silent," reported Meg Cox in the May 19 *Wall Street Journal.*

My point: Big spenders on art works, if they take up coins, will not even flinch at paying $10,000, $25,000, or $100,000 for outstanding specimens of U.S. coins, especially if they are Super Grades. To be sure, they all need not abandon their Rembrandts and van Goghs. But, think how dramatically our market will change if only a few of these high livers develop a minimum degree of passion for rare coins. (A rare U.S. coin has sold for $1.35 million.)

Performance. Let's face it, most of you are interested in the financial aspects of rare coins. That's the audience of the RNA. It says so right on the top of page one. So, let's take a brief look at the record of the detractors to the Super Grades.

Oh yes, there are detractors (far more so than I ever was). Many have strong collector-based businesses and must cater to orders for coins in well circulated grades. They don't want to alienate their customers. Others pooh-pooh 65/better coins saying that they are too speculative, too costly, too thinly supported by misguided investors. I see self-interest in these charges.

One well-known dealer has at several times recommended the purchase of EF Barber halves, among other EF types. He views them as excellent values. You know something? I do, too! I've even recommended certain scarce types in EF and AU grades. But, we must admit two things:

1. What's to prevent EF Barber Halves from appearing to be great values for many years to come? They may remain $100 coins while Super Graded coins soar. Do you want comforting but stagnant value or awesome profits? Look at this ten-year performance record for the EF Barber half using May editions of the *Coin Dealer Newsletter* (wholesale bids):

1978	$75	1982	$105	1986	$100
1980	$80	1983	$100	1988	$100

2. What worked in the last bull market? Was it EF Barber halves? MS-63 Saints? MS-60/62 silver $1 rolls? VF Bust half-dimes? None of the above. It was the Super Graded coins. That's a fact, Jack! That's what worked when the factors you read so far in this report were not present.

*   *   *

A PERFORMANCE COMPARISON OF UNITED STATES
HIGH-GRADE MINT STATE RARE COINS TO UNITED STATES
HIGH-GRADE CIRCULATED RARE COINS

COIN TYPE	1979 MS-65 ASK	1980 MS-65 BID	1979 AU ASK	1980 AU BID
HALF CENTS				
Draped Bust	975	2,500	205	220
Classic	600	1,300	71	70
Braided	580	1,300	77	76
LARGE CENTS				
Draped Bust	*6,600	12,500	510	500
Classic	*8,250	16,000	675	775
Coronet	775	1,150	78	76
Braided	560	1,050	67	65
SMALL CENTS				
Flying Eagle	525	1,150	105	110
Copper-nickel (1859)	525	1,100	100	105
Copper-nickel (1860–64)	150	310	26	25
Indian Head	51	130	9	9
TWO-CENT PIECES	305	700	47	44
THREE-CENT PIECES				
Nickel	195	900	22	21
Silver (I)	455	2,100	78	80
Silver (II)	900	3,350	145	150
Silver (III)	455	2,100	78	80
NICKELS				
Shield (with rays)	900	2,600	130	125
Shield	220	1,400	36	35
Liberty Head (NC)	47	540	8	7
Liberty Head	172	875	24	32
Buffalo (I)	47	310	13	13
HALF-DIMES				
Flowing Hair 1794–5	*9,625	24,000	1,900	3,500

COIN TYPE	1979 MS-65 ASK	1980 MS-65 BID	1979 AU ASK	1980 AU BID
Draped Bust 1796–7	*11,550	35,000	2,450	4,100
Draped Bust 1800–1805	*10,725	28,500	2,050	3,650
Bust	715	3,300	120	165
Liberty Seated (no stars)	1,000	4,500	290	275
Liberty Seated (no drapery)	660	3,300	116	115
Liberty Seated (stars obv.)	550	2,800	83	82
Liberty Seated (arrows)	600	3,000	88	85
Liberty Seated (leg. obv.)	400	2,000	50	52

DIMES

Draped Bust (1796–7)	*9,350	26,000	*3,410	5,750
Draped Bust (1798–1807)	5,600	17,500	1,350	2,500
Bust (large)	1,925	6,000	395	500
Bust (reduced)	1,325	4,200	192	265
Liberty Seated (no stars)	2,250	7,200	460	430
Liberty Seated (no drapery)	825	4,500	110	112
Liberty Seated (stars obv.)	775	3,500	82	82
Liberty Seated (arrows 1853–5)	960	3,700	107	105

COIN TYPE	1984 MS-65 ASK	1985 MS-65 BID	1984 AU ASK	1985 AU BID
Liberty Seated (legend obv.)	375	1,950	38	42
Liberty Seated (arrows 1873–4)	885	4,250	210	210
Barber	275	1,500	28	27
TWENTY-CENT PIECES	1,325	4,000	265	260

QUARTERS

Draped Bust (1796)	*19,250	42,500	*11,000	16,500
Draped Bust (1804–7)	*6,875	20,000	1,450	2,450
Bust (large)	3,000	8,000	630	785
Bust (reduced)	1,875	6,000	310	400
Liberty Seated (no drapery)	*4,400	14,000	255	260
Liberty Seated (no motto)	800	4,100	100	95
Liberty Seated (arrows & rays)	2,600	8,000	210	210
Liberty Seated (arrows 1854–5)	1,225	6,000	187	180
Liberty Seated (with motto)	575	3,700	82	80
Liberty Seated (arrows 1873–4)	1,050	5,000	295	270
Barber	390	2,000	77	75
Standing Liberty (I) Full head	375	1,700	†82	†87

COIN TYPE	1984 MS-65 ASK	1985 MS-65 BID	1984 AU ASK	1985 AU BID
Standing Liberty (II)	137	800	36	45
Standing Liberty (II) Full head	340	1,600	—	—

HALVES

Flowing Hair (1794–5)	*10,500	45,000	2,500	3,350
Draped Bust (1801–7)	*7,000	21,500	675	800
Bust	1,150	3,000	90	105
Bust (reeded edge)	1,925	6,000	290	280
Liberty Seated (no drapery)	*9,000	25,000	785	900
Liberty Seated (no motto)	885	4,650	110	100
Liberty Seated (arrows & rays)	4,250	15,500	475	450
Liberty Seated (arrows 1854–5)	1,350	5,600	195	180
Liberty Seated (with motto)	685	4,300	87	80
Liberty Seated (arrows 1873–4)	1,500	6,000	310	300
Barber	735	4,000	150	155

DOLLARS

Draped Bust (1795–8)	*19,500	52,500	2,100	3,650
Draped Bust (1798–1803)	*12,500	30,000	1,050	1,550
Liberty Seated (no motto)	1,400	3,700	250	275
Liberty Seated (with motto)	1,400	5,000	260	290
Trade	815	3,750	145	160

Note: The *Coin Dealer Newsletter* of March 2, 1979, refers to the highest-quality copper Type coin column as "Ch. BU (MS-65/70)" with a notation that "superb full red (MS-70) specimens often bring far more than prices listed below." However, the highest-quality copper Type coin column in the February 29, 1980, *Coin Dealer Newsletter* carries the label "BU (MS-65)" with the notation that "superb full red (MS-65/70) specimens often bring far more than the prices listed below." Both colums have been listed in the chart above under the MS-65 heading.

COIN TYPE	1984 MS-65 ASK	1985 MS-65 BID	1984 AU ASK	1985 AU BID
HALF CENTS				
Draped Bust	5,000	4,500	340	310
Classic	3,550	2,700	95	87
Braided	3,550	2,800	110	100
LARGE CENTS				
Draped Bust	*12,650	11,500	815	750
Classic	*17,600	16,000	1,085	1,000
Coronet	3,300	2,700	125	120
Braided	2,650	2,500	97	95

COIN TYPE	1984 MS-65 ASK	1985 MS-65 BID	1984 AU ASK	1985 AU BID
SMALL CENTS				
Flying Eagle	2,400	1,900	125	115
Copper-nickel (1859)	2,100	1,475	125	115
Copper-nickel (1860–64)	925	800	32	30
Indian Head	575	330	10	9
TWO-CENT PIECES	1,600	950	52	48
THREE-CENT PIECES				
Nickel	1,075	1,525	31	29
Silver (I)	2,400	3,850	102	95
Silver (II)	3,500	5,000	180	165
Silver (III)	2,300	3,275	108	100
NICKELS				
Shield (with rays)	2,300	3,150	135	125
Shield	1,200	2,100	43	40
Liberty Head (NC)	440	975	10	9
Liberty Head	875	1,600	37	34
Buffalo (I)	155	285	16	15
HALF-DIMES				
Flowing Hair 1794–5	*27,500	25,000	3,000	2,750
Draped Bust 1796–7	*34,100	31,000	3,800	3,500
Draped Bust 1800–1805	*28,600	26,000	2,625	2,400
Bust	4,000	6,100	230	195
Liberty Seated (no stars)	3,950	5,000	310	285
Liberty Seated (no drapery)	3,075	4,850	108	100
Liberty Seated (stars obv.)	2,850	4,350	81	75
Liberty Seated (arrows)	2,850	4,650	81	75
Liberty Seated (legend obv.)	2,100	3,450	49	45
DIMES				
Draped Bust (1796–7)	*33,000	30,000	3,800	3,500
Draped Bust (1798–1807)	*19,800	18,000	1,975	1,800
Bust (large)	*8,690	10,000	625	575
Bust (reduced)	6,400	9,000	360	330
Liberty Seated (no stars)	5,000	5,800	560	510

COIN TYPE	1979 MS-65 ASK	1980 MS-65 BID	1979 AU ASK	1980 AU BID
Liberty Seated (no drapery)	3,550	5,650	125	115
Liberty Seated (stars obv.)	3,150	5,200	79	72
Liberty Seated (arrows 1853–5)	3,150	5,300	97	90
Liberty Seated (legend obv.)	1,650	3,150	44	40
Liberty Seated (arrows 1873–4)	5,000	4,750	245	225
Barber	1,050	1,900	31	29
TWENTY-CENT PIECES	5,000	7,450	325	300
QUARTERS				
Draped Bust (1796)	*44,000	40,000	*12,650	12,500
Draped Bust (1804–7)	*30,250	27,500	2,300	2,100
Bust (large)	*12,100	13,500	1,035	950
Bust (reduced)	8,350	12,000	575	525
Liberty Seated (no drapery)	*13,200	14,000	380	350
Liberty Seated (no motto)	4,400	5,850	97	90
Liberty Seated (arrows & rays)	8,800	8,500	272	250
Liberty Seated (arrows 1854–5)	5,400	6,000	180	165
Liberty Seated (with motto)	2,900	4,725	92	85
Liberty Seated (arrows 1873–4)	4,500	5,000	295	270
Barber	2,150	3,300	82	75
Standing Liberty (I) Full head	1,750	2,375	†87	†80
Standing Liberty (II)	550	1,050	46	42
Standing Liberty (II) Full head	1,750	2,500	—	—
HALVES				
Flowing Hair (1794–5)	*49,500	45,000	3,250	3,000
Draped Bust (1801–7)	*22,000	20,000	1,050	975
Bust	5,250	8,500	210	185
Bust (reeded edge)	7,150	10,000	350	295
Liberty Seated (no drapery)	*22,000	21,500	1,350	1,250
Liberty Seated (no motto)	4,400	6,300	115	105
Liberty Seated (arrows & rays)	14,500	14,000	380	350
Liberty Seated (arrows 1854–5)	6,000	6,800	212	195
Liberty Seated (with motto)	4,125	5,650	103	95
Liberty Seated (arrows 1873–4)	6,200	6,300	350	320
Barber	3,850	5,400	217	200
DOLLARS				
Draped Bust (1795–8)	*49,500	45,000	*9,350	5,000

COIN TYPE	1979 MS-65 ASK	1980 MS-65 BID	1979 AU ASK	1980 AU BID
Draped Bust (1798–1803)	*35,750	32,500	2,850	2,600
Liberty Seated (no motto)	7,200	9,600	410	375
Liberty Seated (with motto)	7,800	9,900	425	390
Trade	4,600	6,500	255	235

* "Bid" plus 10 percent. "Ask" was unlisted because of infrequent trading.

† No listing for full head.

Note: These charts were compiled using price statistics that appeared in the following issues of the *Coin Dealer Newsletter:* March 2, 1979; February 29, 1980; August 31, 1984; and August 30, 1985.

What the Statistical Comparison Shows

The total of the 1979 MS-65 "ask" column is $202,469, and the total of the 1980 MS-65 "bid" column is $602,965, for a 198.7 percent increase over the year.

Realistic Performance of MS-65 Coins During 1979–80

We are able to reach a far more realistic market assessment if we remove the coins valued *above $10,000* from our analysis. Without those late 1970s and early- to mid-1980s resistance-level pieces, the 1979 "ask" is $118,444. And the 1980 "bid" is $369,465. **Thus, the realistic overall market appreciation during that one-year period was approximately 212 percent.**

The Resistance Level

Resistance-level coins are examples that are priced at or near an amount of money considered serious for the period. During the 1990s, that level is around $75,000. As economic variables set in that affect the money supply and consumer spending, the resistance level changes.

In the likely event of inflation, the resistance level can rise to great heights: Perhaps a $10,000 coin of today might be valued at $100,000, $500,000, or much, much, more sometime in the future, as the dollar declines and investors create a great demand for tangible assets.

In the event of inflation, that resistance level would become lower.

The resistance level has historically risen dramatically. Not too long ago that level was $10,000. The resistance level should not be a major factor in long-term investments, for there is every reason to believe that it will continue its historical, upward climb.

Performance of AU-55 Coins During 1979–80

You should be quite concerned how the AUs did. The period from 1979 to 1980 was an exceptional one, and everything did well. The total of the 1979 AU "ask" column is $40,484; and the 1980 AU "bid" column adds up to $58,987. Therefore, those AU coins touted by contrarians increased 45.7 percent over that one-year period. While you might think that 45.7 percent is not too bad, I would rather make 212 percent on my money!

Removing the single coin valued above $10,000 from the 1979 to 1980 AU tabulation results in a 44.1 percent one-year increase figure: the 1979 AU "ask" column totals $29,484, and the 1980 AU "bid" column adds up to $42,487.

Performance of MS-65 Coins During 1984–85
The total of the MS-65 "ask" column for 1984 is $664,535. The total for the MS-65 "bid" column for 1985 is $685,765. Thus, in one year, the entire copper, nickel, and silver business-strike Type column in MS-65 increased about 3.2 percent, taking buy/sell spreads into consideration.

Once again, if we remove those coins valued at above $10,000 from the calculations, the total of the 1984 "ask" column is $199,285 and the total of the 1985 "bid" column is $283,265, for an *approximate one-year appreciation of 42.2 percent*. Remember, we have taken buying and selling commissions into consideration by having used "ask" to reflect the buy price or beginning-of-year valuation and "bid" to reflect the sell price or end-of-year valuation.

During that twelve-month period, therefore, MS-65 business-strike copper, nickel, and silver coins valued at $10,000 or less increased by 42.2 percent, including commissions. Let us take a look at how that compares with the AUs.

Performance of AU-55 Coins During 1984–85
The total of the 1984 AU "ask" column is $61,191, and the 1985 AU "bid" column totals $53,454, for an approximate *loss* of 12.6 percent. If we remove the one coin valued above $10,000 from our AU analysis, the 1984 "ask" column totals $48,541, and the 1985 "bid" column totals $40,954. The *loss,* approximately 15.6 percent, is greater than when the $10,000 is included in the calculations.

It is my opinion that the reason the AU coins performed as well as they did (and still not very well, comparatively) during 1979 to 1980 was that great demand was created by fly-by-night dealers who wanted to cash in on the coin boom and sell AU coins for Mint State prices. These dealers left the field as quickly as they entered it.

The operative word is "quality": no matter how much those AUs and other circulated coins are touted, it is the Mint State coin that usually makes the sale, shows the increase, and rewards its owner with an artistic appreciation of rare coins—and a love for rare coin investing, too!

WHEN TO BUY LESS THAN MINT STATE-64 COINS

There are certain times when you will want to buy MS-63, MS-60, or even lower-grade coins:

- If a coin is so rare in Mint State that it is not available in MS-65, or even in MS-63 or MS-60, then you will have to settle for a coin in a lower (sometimes considerably lower) grade than MS-65. Many early coins, such as coins of the Flowing hair or Bust varieties, are unobtainable or prohibitively expensive in MS-65.
- If the difference in price between MS-63 and MS-65 scares the daylights out of you, and you cannot locate a dealer you are certain is trustworthy, an investment in MS-63 or lower-grade coins might be better than no investment in coins at all.
- If you want to assemble a complete Mint State set, and the prices for a set of all MS-65s are out of your budget, you might want to settle for some MS-63s.
- If a particular area or series is severely depressed and you cannot locate any coins that the dealer believes to be MS-65, but many coins labeled MS-63 or MS-63+ appear to be MS-65 or extremely close, buy them. Those "almost" MS-65s might well trade at MS-65 prices if the market for that area or series picks up.
- If there is a reasonable argument presented for a certain MS-63 increasing in value, give it serious consideration. The general argument that MS-65s have increased at such a high rate that the MS-63s are next is *not* a valid one. Demand moves sideways, not downward. In other words, if someone is buying Barber halves in MS-65, but the MS-65 price increases, say, from $2,000 per coin to $6,000 per coin, that person will not move to MS-63s at, say, $1,500 per coin. Rather, that collector or investor will switch to a more affordable series in MS-65. The grade and high-quality-only obsession does not get compromised; the series does.
- If you are a collector on a budget but are intent on collecting a certain high-priced series, circulated examples might be your only hope of completing the series. There is nothing wrong with this. You can gain the same appreciation of culture, art and history of that coinage design that someone who has a collection worth a multiple of yours can gain.

Do not think that my advice to buy the best is an elitist attitude. I am not telling you to go out and only buy $5,000 and $10,000 coins. There are many coin Types in which the difference between MS-65 and MS-63 is not very great. For example, at the writing of this book, a 1954 Franklin half-dollar in MS-63 is valued at about $14.

Its MS-65 counterpart is worth about $20. As this series becomes more collected and invested in, watch that price spread become much, much larger! It is well worth the extra $6 to have the MS-65.

UNDERVALUED AND OVERVALUED

If you are building a collection of circulated coins, there is no reason to feel that you should stop and begin collecting MS-65s. You are probably collecting for the historical, cultural, and artistic significance, and you are having a great time. So keep on collecting, it's fun!

There is no question that circulated coins are undervalued. But the question everyone wants to know the answer to is: when will the market wake up? Nobody knows. Some things can stay undervalued for years and sometimes never wake up. Others remain dormant for years and suddenly boom.

But just as some coins can be undervalued for an extended period of time, other coins can be *overvalued* for an extended period of time. Will MS-65 fever ever cease? Nobody has a crystal ball (not even this author!) but I can virtually assure you of one thing: there are some overvalued coins out there today that will increase in value dramatically and in ten years be even more overvalued than they are today; and there are some overvalued coins that will decrease dramatically and in ten years be valued at a more realistic level.

The phenomenon of overvaluation is not new. It occurs in any market: it happens with stocks; the art market is not immune to it; and it occurs with real estate. A couple of years ago, a nice New York City two-bedroom cooperative apartment was worth $350,000. As of the writing of this book, it is worth $475,000. There is much talk about New York City real estate being overvalued, but it continues to increase anyway! Buyers do not listen to economic textbooks, and, as a result, many items can stay overvalued for years—just as many items can, and do, remain undervalued for years.

Please note: *The information presented in the preceding chapter is not meant as an endorsement or recommendation* only *of MS-63 or better quality coins. There are many coins of lower grades that make outstanding investments. In fact, some circulated coins are good investments, especially those that have designs that remain attractive even if the coin is well worn (e.g., the Liberty Seated dollar).*

Making a Fortune
Is Conditional*

Marty and Bob were medical school classmates and friends who were both interested in making money from collecting high-quality United States coins. They both appreciated the artistic significance of rare coins, and they were captivated by beautiful coins. Most of all, Marty and Bob were in awe of the appreciation potential that rare United States coins represent.

Both were qualified to be collecting for investment purposes by any prudent person's rule. Marty came from a wealthy family, had a half-million-dollar inheritance from his grandfather, and a huge trust fund upon which his parents allowed him to draw to build his coin collection. Bob had been given $100,000 at the age of eighteen by his father to try out the stock market. By his twentieth birthday, that $100,000 had been turned into nearly $600,000 (after taxes).

Marty started his collection in 1978, right before the great coin boom of 1979 to 1980. He took the time to learn about coin grading and only purchased from reputable dealers. Marty bought most of his coins during a buyers' market, and he used common sense in coin grading. For example, he knew that if a huge gash was visible on the face of a Barber half-dollar, that coin could not possibly be MS-70 or perfect.

Bob developed his interest in rare coins in early 1980 during the

---

* If you have not read the explanation of grading terms contained in chapter 2, you might find it helpful to do so now before you continue. When grading coins, do not use more than a ten-power magnifying glass.

height of the boom, when he and Marty were just beginning their internships at a small Midwestern hospital. Bob, too, learned about coin grading, and he regularly attended public coin auctions so he could see for himself how the crowd reacted to certain coins, as well as observe firsthand what prices were being paid for what coins. Bob, too, only dealt with reputable dealers. But by the time Bob started to collect, Marty had decided not to expand his collection any further. In fact, Marty slowly began to sell off some of his coins in order to liquidate his profits.

Bob was impressed that Marty was able to make a profit from the sale of coins. So Bob increased his rare coin holdings at what neither man realized was the height of the boom.

By the time 1982 had rolled around, Bob had increased his rare coin holdings considerably, and Marty still had a substantial collection. In August of 1982, the coin market showed signs of reawakening, so Marty and Bob decided to sell some of their rare coin holdings.

Once again, Marty made a tidy profit. But Bob was unable to find a buyer for his coins, nor could he find a reputable auction company to grade his coins at the same grade at which he purchased them. Bob's coins were purchased at the height of a boom when grading standard interpretations were loose, due to a lack of high-quality material and intense demand. Although he was certain he got good value when he made his purchases, he did not necessarily receive the near-perfect coins he thought he was purchasing.

Michael Fuljenz sums up this phenomenon in *The Numismatist:*

> From 1979 through the early 80s the coin market was a red-hot seller's market. If many dealers reflect back, they might say that at the time demand was so high that anything round and shiny sold for MS-65 money. . . . It is of utmost importance to realize that at the time, *fair market value* was delivered on wholesale and retail levels in most cases, and that the best descriptions available then had not evolved to represent what those same descriptions signify today. For example, the eagle's breast on the reverse of a Morgan dollar was not examined as closely for bagmarks in 1980 as it is in 1985. Therefore, an MS-65 Morgan dollar of 1980 might only be an MS-63 today because of marks on the eagle's breast. . . . In my opinion, a dealer, collector or investor is being treated fairly as long as fair value is delivered, with accurate descriptions for the time frame.

The only way you can prevent what happened to Bob from happening to you is by consulting a specialist in the series of coin you are considering purchasing. For example, if commemoratives were booming and you wanted to buy some, it would be advisable to speak to someone who specializes in commemoratives and would be able to steer you to issues that would not be perceived to be lower grades if the market were to drop.

Large dealerships sometimes have specialists on staff who can direct you. In many such cases, however, it is your responsibility to read the signals and take the hints. Coin dealerships are out to sell coins. If the numismatist at the firm tells you that a certain coin is not too bad a buy but that he has seen better, take the hint and do not buy the piece being offered.

However, the necessity of your learning at least the basics of coin grading cannot be stressed enough. Small differences in a coin's grade can mean many thousands of dollars. And if you do not know the difference, you could lose a small fortune—or a big one, too!

THE IMPORTANCE OF ACCURATE COIN GRADING

If you wish to profit from your rare coin purchases, nothing is as important as the accurate grading of coins. Although much has been written about counterfeit detection, the coin industry's primary problem remains the need for *both dealers and collectors* to describe the coins they have for sale accurately and ethically.

A dealer friend once remarked that coin grading really is not so subjective. He said that grading is a consensus of subjectivity, which makes it somewhat objective. I agree: in many cases it is not such a subjective judgment whether a coin is a pristine Mint State-65 or a heavily scratched Mint State-60. Dollarwise, the difference is great. Some coin Types have multihundred-percent value differences between Mint State-63 and Mint State-65 listings—or between MS-64 and MS-65 listings!

In many cases, an MS-65 coin might be worth *several hundred percent* of its MS-63 counterpart. To illustrate this, I have prepared a chart of Morgan dollars whose MS-65 values are 800 percent or more of their MS-63 values. This should certainly convince you of the importance of accurate grading!

As with all of the charts in this book, I have strived to be as accurate and realistic as possible. Therefore, I have used the MS-65 "ask" level from the *Coin Dealer Newsletter* to compose the MS-65 column. This is just below the price you would have been likely to pay had you made your purchase in September 1985. But if that "MS-65" turned out to be an MS-63, you might only have been able to receive the MS-63 "bid" price.

MORGAN DOLLARS WHOSE MS-65 VALUES ARE
800 PERCENT OR MORE OF THEIR MS-63 VALUES

VALUES TAKEN FROM THE SEPTEMBER 6, 1985,
COIN DEALER NEWSLETTER

DATE	MS-63 BID	MS-65 ASK
1878 8tf	110	2,150
1878 7/8 8tf	135	2,650
1879	80	1,200
1879-O	150	2,650
1880	82	950
1880-O (8/7)	190	*3,600
1880-O	170	*3,325
1881	80	780
1881-O	80	780
1882	80	775
1884	100	850
1887/6-O	110	*1,900
1887-O	87	1,800
1887-S	210	1,875
1889	80	1,000
1889-O	215	3,150
1890	85	1,225
1890-O	95	1,675
1891	135	2,600
1891-O	175	*4,150
1892-O	350	*3,825
1894-O	950	*14,000
1896-O	1,300	*25,250
1900	75	810
1901	2,100	*25,200
1902	105	1,850
1904	260	2,700
1921	50	680
1921-D	85	1,125
1921-S	95	1,400

* MS-65 "bid" level. There is no listing under MS-65 "ask" for this issue because that coin in this grade is too infrequently traded for a reliable value posting.

Note: The prices indicated here were recorded during a rapid upward adjustment phase of the Morgan dollar market. It is essential that you consult an updated price guide before reaching any value determinations. This chart is intended strictly for educational purposes.

This chart, which indicates the difference in price between MS-63 and MS-65, is not meant to scare you; it is meant to point out the difference that a small variation in grade can make. You probably would not rush out and pay $14,000 for an 1894-O Morgan dollar described as MS-65 even if you collected Morgan dollars and were expert at grading them. But just realizing that the MS-63 example is worth about $950 should encourage you to read and absorb the following pages so that you will understand that there is a noticeable, sometimes *common-sense* difference between the MS-65 coin and its MS-63 counterpart.

The *Coin Dealer Newsletter* lists a column for MS-64, too. Please realize that many Morgan dollars (and Peace dollars*, too) do not quite make the MS-65 grade but are unquestionably better than the usual MS-63. These coins are called MS-64 in the marketplace.

The following descriptions are from *Official A.N.A. Grading Standards for United States Coins* by the American Numismatic Association. The grading standards excerpted here are for Morgan dollars.

Permission for the following to be excerpted was granted by the American Numismatic Association, Colorado Springs, Colorado, copyright holder of the text (copyright © 1981).

Note: Some of these dollars have a prooflike surface. This should be mentioned in any description of such pieces, but the coins should be graded independently of their prooflike quality.

The following test is commonly accepted to determine the prooflike quality of such pieces: place the coin upright at the end of a clearly printed ruler. If the printed lines are observably reflected at a distance of 1 inch to 2 inches, it is called Semi-Prooflike. At 2 inches to 4 inches it is termed Prooflike. Beyond 4 inches is Deep Mirror Prooflike.

MINT STATE *Absolutely no trace of wear.*

MS-70 UNCIRCULATED
A flawless coin exactly as it was minted, with no trace of wear or injury. Must have full mint luster and brilliance or light toning. Any unusual striking traits must be described.

MS-67 UNCIRCULATED
Virtually flawless but with very minor imperfections.

---

* Issued from 1921–35 as commemorative peace coins.

MS-65 UNCIRCULATED
No trace of wear; nearly as perfect as MS-67 except for a few additional minute bag marks or surface mars. Has full mint luster but may be unevenly toned. Any unusual striking traits must be described.

MS-63 UNCIRCULATED
A mint state coin with attractive mint luster, but noticeable detracting contact marks or minor blemishes.

MS-60 UNCIRCULATED
A strictly Uncirculated coin with no trace of wear, but with bag marks and other abrasions more obvious than for MS-63. May have a few small rim mars and weakly struck spots. Has full mint luster but may lack brilliance, and surface may be spotted or heavily toned.

Business strike silver dollars were all placed in mint bags of 1,000 coins. Subsequent handling of bags caused bag marks and abrasions on virtually all coins, which are not to be confused with circulation wear. Full mint luster and lack of any wear are necessary to distinguish MS-60 from AU-55.

Check points for signs of wear: hair above eye and ear, edges of cotton leaves and bolls, high upper fold of cap; high points of eagle's breast and tops of legs. Weakly struck spots are common and should not be confused with actual wear.

ABOUT UNCIRCULATED *Small trace of wear visible on highest points.*

AU-55 *Choice*
OBVERSE: Slight trace of wear shows on hair above ear, eye, edges of cotton leaves, and high upper fold of cap. Luster fading from cheek.
REVERSE: Slight trace of wear shows on breast, tops of legs and talons.

Most of the mint luster is still present, although marred by light bag marks and surface abrasions.

AU-50 *Typical*
OBVERSE: Traces of wear show on hair above eye, ear, edges of cotton leaves, and high upper fold of cap. Partial detail visible on tops of cotton bolls. Luster gone from cheek.
REVERSE: There are traces of wear on breast, tops of legs, wing tips and talons.

Fig. 6–1. *MS-65* 1853 Large cent. This is a lightly fingermarked but Choice coin.

Fig. 6–2. *MS-63* 1854 Large cent. Spots prevent this coin from being an MS-65.

Fig. 6–3. *MS-65* 1902 Indian head cent. Beautiful color and surfaces combine to make this a Choice example.

Fig. 6–4. *MS-63* 1909-S Indian head cent. The uneven toning makes this coin a strong MS-63.

Fig. 6–5. *MS-65* 1909-S Lincoln head cent. The stunning original surfaces and freedom from spots help this coin qualify for the MS-65 designation.

Fig. 6–6. *MS-63* 1955 Doubled die Lincoln head cent. The uneven oxidation of the cheek and jawbone reduce the grade to MS-63. The darker color of the high points is *not* wear.

Fig. 6–7. *Proof-65* 1873 two-cent piece. Unusually problem-free surfaces make this a Choice example.

Fig. 6–8. *Proof-63* 1873 two-cent piece. The oxidized surfaces reduce the grade to 63.

Fig. 6–9. *Proof-65* 1889 copper-nickel three-cent piece. The cameo contrast and lack of carbon spots help this coin rate a full Proof-65. Notice the knife-edge rim, which helps to confirm the Proof status.

Fig. 6–10. *Proof-63* 1887/6 copper-nickel three-cent piece. A particularly detracting spot beneath the eye is a contributing factor in the assignment of the 63 grade.

Fig. 6–11. *Proof-60* 1886 copper-nickel three-cent piece. Rim corrosion and a somewhat dingy appearance force the downgrading of this Proof to the 60 designation.

Fig. 6–12. *Proof-65* 1880 Shield nickel. An amazing example with a stunning cameo contrast.

Fig. 6–13. *Proof-63* 1878 Shield nickel. Surface dullness and lack of universal aesthetic appeal cause this coin to rate as a Proof-63. Nevertheless, it is relatively problem-free.

Fig. 6–14. *Proof-65* 1910 Liberty head nickel. Streaky russet toning upon a delightful cameo helps to create that magically appealing look.

Fig. 6–15. *Proof-63* 1903 Liberty head nickel. Scattered blemishes place this otherwise 65 coin in the 63 category.

Fig. 6–16. *Proof-65* 1937 Buffalo nickel. The brilliant surfaces and lack of hairlines give this coin much appeal.

Fig. 6–17. *Proof-63* 1937 Buffalo nickel. A single rim nick at 12:00 removes this coin from the Choice category. A second nick at 11:00 keeps this coin far away from the Proof-65 price.

Fig. 6–18. *MS-65* 1925-S Mercury dime. This example possesses mark-free, satinlike luster.

Fig. 6–19. *MS-63* 1942/1 Mercury dime. Notice the spotty toning areas.

Fig. 6–20. *Proof-60* 1875 twenty-cent piece. Extensive hairline scratches prevent this coin from even rating Proof-63. The hairlines are most visible in the right field, as indicated by the arrow.

Fig. 6–21. *Proof-65* 1890 Liberty Seated quarter. This spectacular cameo example amazes even a nonnumismatist. A Mint-made imperfection does not subtract from the numerical grade.

Fig. 6–22. *Proof-63* 1872 Liberty Seated quarter. Scattered spots and uneven toning reduce the eye-appeal of this coin.

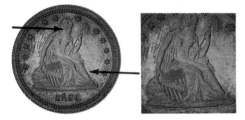

Fig. 6–23. *Proof-60* 1866 Liberty Seated quarter (enlarged). Awesome original toning, but gashes through cheek and leg, as well as scattered hairline scratches in the right field, reduce the grade to Proof-60.

Fig. 6–24. *Mint State* 1873 with arrows Liberty Seated half. An absolutely amazing Mint State example with beaming Mint luster.

Fig. 6–25. *About Uncirculated* 1884 Liberty Seated half. An extremely deceptive example that might appear to be Mint State. Wear is particularly evident on the left breast, knee, and hand, where the arrows are pointing.

Fig. 6–26. *Proof-65* 1880 Liberty Seated half. A breathtakingly beautiful example with a sky-blue and royal chestnut periphery.

Fig. 6–27. *Proof-63* 1883 Liberty Seated half. A most attractive and original coin with that magically "right" appearance but with detractions that cause a downgrading to 63. The lighter color on the high points is not wear.

Fig. 6–28. *Proof-65* 1892 Barber half. This is an example of an aesthetic knockout. Splashes of ocean-blue, rose-red, violet, and sunset-gold combine to make this example particularly alluring.

Fig. 6–29. *Proof-63* 1895 Barber half. A dazzling cameo is no assurance of Proof-65 quality, as this hairlined half demonstrates.

Fig. 6–30. *EF-45* 1836 Liberty Seated dollar. The wear is indicated by the arrows.

Fig. 6–31. *MS-65* 1885-CC Morgan dollar. An incredible, strong MS-65. Notice the near-perfect cheek and well-struck hair above the ear.

Fig. 6–32. *ANACS graded "MS-65, weakly struck"* 1921-S Morgan dollar. This coin might not even be worth the prices listed for MS-60. (ANACS photograph)

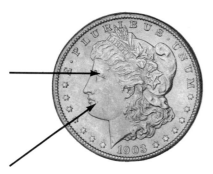

Fig. 6–33. *MS-63* 1903-S Morgan dollar. Detracting marks on the cheek and above the eye, as indicated by the arrows, remove this coin from the MS-65 category.

Fig. 6–34. *MS-60* 1893-0 Morgan dollar. A facial gash keeps this specimen well within the MS-60 grade.

Fig. 6–35. *AU-55* 1889-CC Morgan dollar. An extremely deceptive coin that appears to be Mint State at first glance, but upon close inspection can be seen to display light "rubbing."

Fig. 6–36. *EF-40* 1893-S Morgan dollar. Not too many scratches are visible because this coin displays extensive wear.

Fig. 6–37. *MS-63* 1884 Morgan dollar, reverse. Charcoal-gray toning and scattered marks cause a grade of MS-63. (ANACS photograph)

Fig. 6–38. *AU-50* 1882 Morgan dollar, reverse. Although the color may appear similar to the MS-63 reverse, this reverse displays extensive wear. Notice the rubbing throughout the fields. (ANACS photograph)

Fig. 6–39. *Proof-65* 1885 Morgan dollar. Splendid autumn-leaf and golden-russet toning with splashes of cherry-red, ocean-blue, and violet help give this coin utterly dynamic eye-appeal.

Fig. 6–40. *Proof-63* 1895 Morgan dollar. Various detractions, as indicated by the arrows, remove this coin from the 65 category.

Fig. 6–41. *MS-65* 1934 Peace dollar. The fortuitous escape from injury and scratches makes this example particularly sought-after.

Fig. 6–42. *MS-63* 1928 Peace dollar. The scratches, not the toning, place this coin in the MS-63 category.

Fig. 6–43. *Mint State* 1875-S Trade dollar. No wear is visible on this beautiful original Uncirculated example.

Fig. 6–44. *About Uncirculated* 1878-S Trade dollar. The luster is interrupted, and this coin displays extensive signs of rubbing and handling. The color is pretty, but the coin is an AU.

Fig. 6–45. *Proof-65* 1879 Trade dollar. An awesome cameo contrast between the mirrorlike fields and snow-white devices helps this coin achieve the 65 status. Slight striking weakness of the head and stars does not downgrade this piece.

Fig. 6–47. *Proof-65* 1870 Coronet quarter-eagle.

Fig. 6–46. *Proof-63* 1882 Trade dollar. This coin is prevented from being graded Proof-65 by the three field digs, as indicated by the arrows.

Fig. 6–49. *Proof-60* 1892 Coronet quarter-eagle. Various problems cause the assigned grade.

Fig. 6–48. *Proof-63* 1895 Coronet quarter-eagle. Scattered field digs prevent a Proof-65 grade. Otherwise, this coin has the right look for a 65.

Fig. 6–50. *Proof-55* 1891 Coronet quarter-eagle. Rubbing is visible throughout this piece, particularly in the fields.

Fig. 6–51. *AU-55* 1801 Capped bust eagle. Many coins like this one are described as Mint State and sold for high prices. Notice the wear on the highest points; the color is lighter on those points.

Fig. 6–52. *MS-64* 1901-S Coronet eagle. This piece is controversial, as many experts would grade it MS-65. Nevertheless, it has some scratches, as indicated by the arrows.

Fig. 6–53. *MS-60* 1893 Coronet eagle. Multiple marks cause this coin to rank as an MS-60.

Fig. 6–54. *About Uncirculated* 1853-0 Coronet eagle. Again, signs of wear are most visible in the fields, indicating that the coin has been circulated.

Fig. 6–55. *MS-64* 1884-CC Liberty head double-eagle. Rim problems and light facial scratches cause the assignment of the MS-63 grade to an otherwise MS-65 coin.

Fig. 6–56. *AU-55* 1855-S Liberty head double-eagle. The luster is interrupted, and wear is evident.

Fig. 6–57. *EF-45* 1876-CC Liberty head double-eagle. This coin has little luster but displays a smooth appearance. That is because it has been well worn.

Fig. 6–58. *Proof-65* 1890 Liberty head double-eagle. This coin is a phenomenal attention-getter because of its cameo contrast and overall visual appeal.

Fig. 6–59. *Proof-64* 1899 Liberty head double-eagle. This coin is also a phenomenal attention-getter but has light facial scratches that grab the grader's attention. The grade is close to 65.

Fig. 6–60. *Proof-63* 1903 Liberty head double-eagle. This coin is unquestionably a 63. The appearance is spotty.

Fig. 6–61. *Proof-60 (at best)* 1906 Liberty head double-eagle. This proof is no better than a 60 and might be accurately classified as impaired because of the extensive contact marks.

Fig. 6–62. *MS-65* 1908 without motto Saint-Gaudens double-eagle. This virtually superb coin is head-and-shoulders above what is often offered as MS-65. Notice the lack of scratches on the breasts and knee.

Fig. 6–63. *MS-63* 1909-D Saint-Gaudens double-eagle. This coin absolutely does not qualify for the MS-65 grade, although many like it are sold as MS-65s. Notice the scattered marks.

Fig. 6–64. *AU-55* 1925-S Saint-Gaudens double-eagle. This coin represents the "slider" class. It is attractive but has extensive rubbing.

Three-quarters of the mint luster is still present. Surface abrasions and bag marks are more noticeable than for AU-55.

EXTREMELY FINE *Very light wear on only the highest points.*

EF-45   *Choice*
OBVERSE: Slight wear on hair above date, forehead and ear. Lines in hair well detailed and sharp. Slight flat spots on edges of cotton leaves. Minute signs of wear on cheek.
REVERSE: High points of breast are lightly worn. Tops of legs and right wing tip show wear. Talons are slightly flat.
Half of the mint luster is still present.

EF-40   *Typical*
OBVERSE: Wear shows on hair above date, forehead and ear. Lines in hair well defined. Flat spots visible on edges of cotton leaves. Cheek lightly worn.
REVERSE: Almost all feathers gone from breast. Tops of legs, wing tips and feathers on head show wear. Talons are flat.
Partial mint luster is visible.

Although the A.N.A. standards excerpted above apply to Morgan dollars, the language is almost identical in descriptions of other United States coin Types. Carefully study the A.N.A.'s grading guidelines. They are as close as this field has come to an industry grading standard. You will learn how to comprehend and apply the A.N.A.'s grading system more fully in the sections that follow.

Steve Ivy and Ron Howard, writing in *What Every Silver Dollar Buyer Should Know* (The Ivy Press, 1984), have provided precise definitions for MS-65 and MS-63 Morgan dollars, reproduced in part here.

MS-65   A dollar that may have small bagmarks widely scattered across the surfaces, or several bagmarks longer than the width of a single denticle, but not both. The cheek of Ms. Liberty may have some small marks, but cannot have any major injuries, such as a deep scratch or a prominent milling mark. The breast of the eagle should be perfect or very nearly so. The rims may have one or two imperfections, but they must not extend more than halfway between the edge of the coin and the bottom of the denticles. The luster must be full and unbroken. If there are slide marks, they must be minor, and be virtually the only defect on the obverse of the coin. A dollar with slide marks and more than a few sparse bagmarks cannot be graded MS-65. Any toning will not reduce or improve the grade, but should be mentioned when describing the coin. An MS-65 dollar should be pleasant in its overall appearance. A single major mark can be enough to remove a dollar from the MS-65 level. An MS-65 dollar must be fully struck.

MS-63   A dollar with numerous small bagmarks (those no longer than the width of a single denticle at its midpoint), or a few serious bagmarks, but not both. Liberty's cheek should not have any serious injuries, nor should the eagle's breast, though both of these areas may show some bagmarks and/or abrasions. The rims may have some nicks and dents, but none should extend into the denticles. The luster must be unbroken, although it may not be as intense and vibrant as that on an MS-65 or better coin. An MS-63 dollar must be fully struck unless it otherwise qualifies as an MS-65. Any significant toning should be mentioned.

Although, in one sense, Ivy and Howard can be viewed as interpreting A.N.A. standards, in another sense they are stating marketplace standards, not textbook standards. In particular, Ivy and Howard state that a Morgan dollar has to be fully struck to be graded MS-65. The A.N.A. believes that strike has nothing to do with grade, as will be further discussed. Some experts believe that grading standards of Morgan dollars have tightened since the Ivy/Howard book was written. Nevertheless, Ivy and Howard should be commended for adding specificity to the standards of grading by so clearly defining requirements in their book.

A MULTIMILLION-DOLLAR COIN-GRADING LESSON

The building of grading skill requires book knowledge combined with practical experience. It is easy for you to pick up a copy of the A.N.A.'s grading guide and read through some of the descriptions, as well as look at the line drawings. But it is not as easy to acquire practical experience—or at least it is not as cheap! What practical experience too often means is that if you buy a coin for $100 and find out later that you should have paid no more than $50, you have learned a valuable lesson.

Walter H. Breen, the celebrated numismatic scholar, has this to say about how some coin buyers learn: "The novice who spends tens of thousands of dollars on coins is getting a very expensive education. What many of them learn that way is that they've been swindled."

Although there are many reputable dealers from whom you can safely purchase coins, there are some dealers from whom you should not purchase. Some telemarketing firms, for example, cannot even be trusted with your credit-card number. That is why you need to arm yourself. Knowledge is power, and you need to become as knowledgeable as possible about grading.

The coins you will probably be purchasing, even if you are a collector with no interest in investment, are the coins in the highest grades—the Mint State coins. These are the coins you need to study and learn about. You literally *cannot afford not to know how to grade Mint State coins.* Slight variations in grade can mean thousands of dollars in value. And if you pay $30,000 for a coin that you think is a Proof-65 double-eagle gold piece but that turns out to be nothing better than a Proof-60 worth $6,000, then you have paid $24,000 to find out the difference between a Proof-60 and its Proof-65 counterpart!

The color photographs in this section are designed to show you how to grade Mint State coins as well as to identify coins that might appear to be Mint State, but are not. Each coin illustration, with the exception of three Morgan dollar photos taken by the American Numismatic Association Certification Service, was made available for this project courtesy of Heritage Capital Corporation.

The Heritage firm spent over three months compiling 116 eight-inch by ten-inch transparencies, which were used since 1982 in both the firm's auction and retail divisions. Each transparency page contained reproductions of approximately thirty coins. The coin photographs appearing in the color grading section in this book were selected from a total of nearly 4,000 coin pictures. The total combined value of the 4,000 coins is several million dollars.

The Heritage companies have the most sophisticated photographic equipment in use in the collectibles field as of the writing of this book. The firm uses a Hasselblad camera and at least thirty different pieces of support equipment. The system was custom-designed over a six-month period in 1979.

The coin photographs in this section, with the exception of the photos taken by ANACS, have been labeled with the same grades assigned to them by the Heritage staff. If, while searching for suitable coins to illustrate this chapter, I found a particular coin graded as, say, MS-63, but I believed that the coin looked like an MS-65 from the photograph, I did not use that photograph. This reverse is also true: if a coin was labeled EF-45 by Heritage but would appear to my readers from the photograph to be an EF-40, the photo was not used.

I am not stating that Heritage has mislabeled any photographs. I am saying that the photographs used in this chapter were selected strictly for educational purposes and in most cases without my having seen the actual coin. **No representation as to actual grade is made as to the coins shown in these photographs.**

Since only obverses of the coins are displayed, only the obverse grade has been used. For example, if a particular coin was labeled by Heritage as MS-65/63, I have only displayed the MS-65 obverse grade because you cannot see the reverse and, therefore, that grade would be irrelevant.

This grading lesson has been broken down by metallic category for ease of imparting information. The photographs and accompanying explanations should be adequate for you to realize, at the very least, that there is no real mystique behind grading and that, to a very large degree, it is merely common sense. If you learn from this chapter even one grading "lesson," you will have more than paid for the cost of this book. And if you learn more than one grading lesson, you might just profit enough from rare coin purchases to pay for your children's college education. The number and value of the coins from which these photos were selected, as well as the potential they have of educating you, truly make this a multimillion-dollar coin-grading lesson.

Identification of MS-65 Coins
It is extremely important to be able to identify MS-65 coins confidently. Too often, the novice believes either that large gouges have little impact on a coin's grade or that MS-65 coins have to be perfect. Both points of view can be dangerous. A coin with large scratches cannot possibly be MS-65 and often only qualifies for MS-60. And limiting your acquisitions to coins that appear perfect would mean that you would have a mighty small collection indeed.

Many times I have seen novices not buy a reasonably priced coin offered to them that had one or two tiny marks and was graded MS-65—only to buy an AU-55 with no marks at the MS-65 price!

Copper Coins

Braided Hair Large Cents
The 1853 Braided hair large cent, which grades MS-65 (fig. 6-1), is *not* a perfect coin. But it is an MS-65, and it does not have to be perfect. Sure, it is lightly fingermarked. But *Official A.N.A. Grading Standards for United States Coins* states that this type "may be

unevenly toned or lightly fingermarked." Notice the beautiful original color.

At the time of the writing of this book, the market for copper coins is not active. Therefore, although this coin may technically qualify for the MS-65 grade, it probably would not command an MS-65 price among dealers. If copper coins were suddenly to boom, this coin might be valued at the MS-65 price-guide valuations.

The 1854 Braided hair large cent (fig. 6-2) has spots that prevent it from being assigned an MS-65 designation. The color is original, however, and no major nicks or gashes are present. Furthermore, the cheek and most of the head—important grade-sensitive areas—are free from spots. The large, black spot at 12:00, as indicated by the arrow, is referred to as a "carbon" spot, although the spot is not really made of carbon but is merely a darkened toning area. Such "mishandling" spots occur when a coin is spoken over and saliva lands on the coin. Most MS-60s are red and brown and have major detracting marks. The same standards that apply to large cents also apply to half cents.

Indian Head Cents
In figure 6-3, a 1902 Indian head cent with original color is displayed. Beware of any bright Indian cent: many have been dipped (a coin is considered to have been "dipped" when it has been placed in a solution engineered to remove oxidation or light tarnish). Copper coins are the easiest to detect if they have been cleaned in any way, because of their delicacy of color.

The 1909-S (the "S" is on the reverse) Indian head cent shown in figure 6-4 is somewhat heavily fingermarked, with light spotting. The color is original, though. The fingermarking is well defined; therefore, that darker, brownish color is not wear or what is referred to as "rub." (A coin with a rub has been lightly circulated and has been merely "rubbed" by, perhaps, perspiration-soaked fingers.)

Lincoln Head Cents
The 1909-S Lincoln head cent in MS-65 (fig. 6-5) is a first-rate original example. Nineteen hundred and nine was the first year of issue for the Lincoln cent, and many 1909 Lincolns are therefore available in the original level of preservation because the public has a habit of saving first-year-of-issue coins because those coins look interesting. Copper is extremely susceptible to carbon or darkened toning spots and should be examined closely for such spots. When the Lincoln cent is graded, particular emphasis should be placed on examining both the cheek and jawbone. If the coin were to have experienced wear, those areas of wear would be of a different color than the rest of the coin.

The darkened color on the highest points of the 1955 doubled die Lincoln cent in figure 6-6 is not wear but, rather, oxidation resulting from the coin having moved around in a paper envelope. Wear is identified by a break in a coin's luster. If this coin were to be tilted and rotated under a pinpoint light source, such as a Tensor or high-intensity lamp, the light would be reflected off those high points in a *circular pattern.* (Methods of identifying a coin with wear will be discussed below.) By the way, the doubling on this coin should be clearly visible. Such doubling is caused by the *dies* having been struck twice, not the coin.

Two-Cent Pieces

The 1873 two-cent piece displayed in figure 6-7 is a brilliant and highly desirable example. This coin is a Proof—a coin struck twice on specially polished dies and specially selected planchets to assure a chromiumlike brilliance. The fields—the coin's background—are reflective; and the devices—the parts that stand out from the coin or are raised above the surface—are frosted. The contrast between those frosted devices and reflective fields is referred to as a "cameo" contrast.

The other 1873 two-cent piece in Proof (fig. 6-8) has rather dark toning as well as some carbon spots. When a coin is toned, always try to look beneath the toning. This example is a Proof-63 because of the spots, as well as the dark color. As a rule, however, toning does not add to or subtract from the numerical grade; it merely has an impact on the value. Some extraordinary toning may boost a grade in marginal cases, and this will be discussed later. In the marketplace, a darkened copper coin is rarely considered MS-65.

Toning and Tarnish. It should be understood that *toning* is a slow process that occurs over a period of months and years. The toning on the 1873 Proof-63 two-cent piece is referred to as "patina." *Tarnishing* is a quick and irregular process that occurs over a short period of time, perhaps weeks or even days. Toning has little or no impact on grade, except on copper coins.

Copper-Nickel Coins

The three-cent nickel piece, which is popularly referred to as the copper-nickel three-cent piece, is composed primarily of copper (75 percent copper; 25 percent nickel). However, the coin itself is generally white in appearance, although it acquires unsightly spots similar to those detracting spots on copper coins. The three-cent nickel, however, has the same copper-nickel combination (75 percent copper; 25 percent nickel) as the nickel five-cent piece. Other coins composed of a copper and nickel combination include the Flying Eagle cent and the Indian Head cent issues of 1859 through 1864 (88 percent copper; 12 percent nickel).

Three-Cent Nickels
The splendid example of a Proof-65 1889 three-cent nickel piece (fig. 6-9) displays a remarkable cameo contrast. It is also fairly free from spots. The knife-edge rims, as indicated by the arrow, are a contributing factor in confirming this coin's Proof status.

The Proof-63 three-cent nickel displayed in figure 6-10 also displays a cameo contrast but the darkened toning spot beneath the eye removes this piece from the Proof-65 category. There are also various other detracting spots. This coin was struck from the 1886 die, which was later reëngraved with a "7." This variety is referred to as the "1887 over 6."

The Proof-60 grade is often assigned to a coin for its generally dingy and unattractive appearance, sometimes combined with other factors. The 1886 Proof-60 three-cent nickel shown in figure 6-11 is one such example. The coin is generally dingy, and there is evidence of corrosive porosity on the rim, where the arrow is pointing. We can be reasonably convinced of this coin's Proof status because only Proofs were struck of the three-cent nickel bearing the 1886 date.

Nickel Coins

Shield Nickels
The breathtaking 1880 Shield nickel graded Proof-65 (fig. 6-12) is another stunning cameo specimen. There is a trace of light golden toning, and the toning areas within the shield and by the date have no effect on the grade. The right side appears darker than the left because of the lighting.

The 1878 Shield nickel graded Proof-63 (fig. 6-13) has no major detractions, but its visual appeal leaves much to be desired. The coin appears rather dull and may have been cleaned. This Shield nickel is a good demonstration of the fact that grading is often a product of intuitive feel. Although this coin may appear to be a Proof-65, it is not.

Liberty Head Nickels
The streaky-russet-toned 1910 Liberty head nickel (fig. 6-14) is another coin that requires an intuitive feel in order to appreciate its quality. This example is truly a premium specimen. Take note of the cameo contrast, the needle-sharp strike, and the fully rounded block

rims. The light toning areas do not penetrate the coin's surface and, thus, the grade is not affected.

The 1903 Liberty head nickel shown in figure 6-15 is not an undesirable coin, but it has some detractions visible to the naked eye that are not allowable on the Proof-65. Furthermore, this coin may have been dipped—something that has to be sensed and may not be provable.

Buffalo Nickels

The 1937 Buffalo nickel (referred to as such because of a Buffalo on the reverse, which cannot be seen here) in figure 6-16 is a fully brilliant Proof-65. The single toning spot in the hair does not cause this coin to be downgraded.

The other 1937 Buffalo nickel in Proof (fig. 6-17) is not graded Proof-65. There are three rim nicks—the center one located at 12:00, as indicated by the arrow—that remove this coin from the 65 category. Although such a coin might ordinarily qualify for a Proof-65 grade, if the rim has more than one small nick, it might be graded lower.

Silver Coins

Mercury Dimes and Twenty-Cent Pieces

Toning Spots and Hairlines. The 1925-S Mercury dime (fig. 6-18) has a delightful satinlike luster and full Mint brilliance. It is most attractive, original, and has few detractions. Again, there are light toning areas that do not penetrate the coin's surface and, therefore, do not subtract from the grade. But the other Mercury dime (fig. 6-19), which happens to be the scarce overdate variety, 1942 over 1, grades MS-63. The MS-63 is somewhat spotty and, therefore, does not qualify for a higher grade. Furthermore, one spot, as indicated by the arrow, actually penetrates the coin's surface.

But do not think spots that eat into the surface or very noticeable gashes or gouges are the only grade-detracting marks that Mint State coins possess. Just because a coin is brilliant, has no wear, and is well struck does not mean that it automatically qualifies for a high Mint State grade. The 1875 twenty-cent piece Proof in figure 6-20 is a coin that at first might appear to be a Proof-65—or even better. But this coin has multiple hairline scratches, as indicated by the arrow, especially prominent in the right obverse field.

Hairlines are light scratches that occur as the result of light friction—perhaps merely one gentle wipe with a facial tissue. These lines can be especially detracting to Proofs. Do not confuse hairlines, which are surface impairments, with *die polishing marks,* which are raised marks that the coin is manufactured with.

Liberty Seated Quarters

How to Evaluate Surfaces. The 1890 Liberty Seated quarter (fig. 6-21), graded Proof-65, is a stunning and awesome cameo specimen. The coin possesses a full cameo appearance: the devices are fully frosted, and the fields have a mirrorlike reflectivity. The coin was apparently struck with the imperfection that appears at 8:45. Sometimes a piece of lint is struck into the coin and a mark results. This is referred to as a "lint mark" and would detract slightly from the price, but not the grade.

The 1872 Liberty Seated quarter (fig. 6-22) is quite attractive, even though it is not a Proof-65. However, while it is graded Proof-63 and has the visual appeal of a 63, you should still look beneath the toning for signs of more severe damage. Proof-63s are often found with hairlines, although in the photograph, this coin does not show signs of hairlines. The royal chestnut color, however, distracts you from the scattered toning spots that apparently *penetrate the surface*.

Some coins are so beautiful and are toned in such breathtaking, hypnotic, and original colors that you are almost tempted to assign a 67 grade at first glance. The 1866 Liberty Seated quarter (fig. 6-23) is one such coin. The overall visual appeal is awesome. The coin has fully squared-off rims and a full strike, indicating beyond a reasonable doubt that it is a Proof. The crescent of violet that graces the obverse focuses attention on the toning and diverts attention from closely examining the surfaces. However, the coin has some hidden flaws.

Let us look at it more closely: there is a huge gash across Miss Liberty's face; there is a nick on the knee; and there are some hairlines, most visible in the photograph in the right field. Furthermore, there appears to be a rim problem at 10:00, although not enough conclusions can be drawn from the photo for an adequate description. But there is enough information for us to draw the conclusion that this coin does not grade Proof-67 or Proof-65. It cannot qualify for the Proof-63 grade because there are just too many problems. This coin has to be graded Proof-60, although it will certainly trade in the marketplace for well above the average Proof-60 price.

Liberty Seated Half-Dollars

How to Tell the Difference between A.U. and B.U. The attractive, untoned 1873 with arrows Liberty Seated half-dollar (fig. 6-24) is displayed to illustrate what an unquestionable Mint State business-strike Liberty Seated half looks like. There is no need to be concerned about any fine distinctions of this coin's Mint State grade at this time. Just observe the beaming luster, especially on such areas as the left knee and the left hand.

Now look at the 1884 Liberty Seated half-dollar, graded About Uncirculated (fig. 6-25). There is light wear on the highest points, as indicated by the arrows. You must be careful not to mistake specimens such as this one for Mint State. Sometimes novices see a coin such as this one, are pleased that it is bright and has few scratches, and pay a hefty Mint State price for it. *You literally cannot afford to think that this coin is Mint State! It Is About Uncirculated.* It makes no difference that this coin is bright and sharp. It has been spent, circulated, and passed from hand to hand. Carefully study and compare this coin to the Mint State 1873 with arrows half.

Proof Liberty Seated Half-Dollars

The Liberty Seated half-dollar in Proof-65 is a popular investment Type coin, but few are as attractive as the 1880 shown in figure 6-26. A legitimate feeling of originality is created by the electric blue and rose-russet peripheral toning, which fades into a silver-gray center. If we were to assume that this coin is hairline free, then it would be a strong Proof-65.

Proof versus Business Strike. Pay particular attention to the needle-sharp strike and knife-edge rims characteristic of a Proof on that 1880 half. Now compare the bold strike, knife-edge rims and overall appearance to the appearance of the 1873 business strike half in figure 6-24. The difference between the Proof and the business strike should be noticeable. The rims of the 1873 are visibly rounded. If you were to actually examine both coins, you would be able to appreciate the mirrorlike fields and frosted devices of the Proof and compare those characteristics to the luster and nonreflective surfaces exhibited by the business strike.

Subtle Grading Differences of Expensive Type Coins. The 1883 Liberty Seated half, graded Proof-63 (fig. 6-27), is a highly attractive coin. The sky-blue toning about Miss Liberty is original, and the lighter color of the high points is not wear. This coin is originally toned and may have moved around in a paper envelope. Nevertheless, that lighter high-point color has no influence over this coin's Proof-63 grade. This coin is another example of the use of intuition in coin grading. This half apparently has some light hairlines that are not too visible in the photograph, although if you examine the right field carefully you should be able to detect them.

Closely examine any toning that looks like the toning around the date of the 1883 half. Sometimes this area is actually corrosive porosity that looks like toning or even a removable matter, but in fact the coin's surface has been penetrated.

Original and Artificial Toning. Toning is a process that occurs over an extended period of time. Toning that is *original,* and not induced by means of any artificial chemical process, often adds substantially to a coin's aesthetic appeal and, thus, its value.

The most important factor to consider when viewing toned coins is what is beneath the toning. Toning has been known to cover a multitude of sins: scratches, scrapes, hairlines, spots, reëngraving and many other imperfections. Although toning usually does not detract from the grade, it can cover up imperfections that do detract. *The only way you can become accustomed to originally toned coins is by viewing coins in quantity and gaining an intuitive feel for what the original and the artificial look like.*

One of the problems with toned coins is the lack of agreement that often results because of the toning. In recent years, many coins have been artificially toned, and some dealers have been fooled by the toning—toning that often masks imperfections. As a result, many dealers (and collectors, too!) believe that almost any coin with rich toning has been artificially toned.

Barber Half-Dollars

The wondrous 1892 Barber half-dollar in Proof-65 (fig. 6-28) exhibits splashes of ocean-blue and violet about a sunset-golden center. This is what it takes to be a Proof-65 Barber: mark-free surfaces, fully squared-off block rims, spectacular contrast between the fields and the devices, and a phenomenal color that exudes originality and artistic appeal. If you did not appreciate the artistic aspect of rare coins, you should after having looked at this photograph!

Not all flashy cameo coins can automatically be given the 65 grade. The Proof-63 1895 Barber half-dollar (fig. 6-29) is one such coin. There are numerous hairlines and other detracting marks. One line in particular, in front of the mouth, stands out. Nevertheless, the coin is still gorgeous. Just realize that it is not a Proof-65 and appreciate its beauty after you have paid a Proof-63 price.

The Grading of Dollars

Early dollars are quite rare in Mint State. However, numerous coin buyers insist on the purchase of Mint State early-date dollars for their collections and investment portfolios. This intense pressure may cause some coin sellers to push up slightly the grade of some coins that have wear to a Mint State grade. Again, scrutinize the highest points. Check for wear. Look beneath the toning.

Some circulated early dollars even have the same type of attractive toning that Mint State coins do. Just because a coin has attractive toning does not mean that it is Mint State. The 1836 Gobrecht dollar (fig. 6-30) has attractive peripheral toning. But the coin grades Extremely Fine-45! This specimen was part of publishing magnate Amon Carter's collection and developed the toning over many years.

Morgan Dollars

Silver dollars are large and were originally transported by bag, which caused many of the dollars to hit against each other and create "bagmarks" on the coins. Consequently, silver dollars with no marks or imperfections of any kind are extremely rare and sought after.

MS-65. The 1885-CC Morgan dollar, graded MS-65 (fig. 6-31), has virtually no marks or imperfections of any kind and almost qualifies for a higher grade. Do not nitpick and try to find some flaws. They are minor. Morgan dollars such as this are scarce, and feverish demand has always persisted for them. Also, the strike is excellent, and the hair above the ear is well struck. If you see a Morgan dollar this nice or close to it, an MS-65 grade assignation is probably in order.

ANACS "MS-65 Weakly struck." Not all MS-65s are created equal. That incredible 1885-CC MS-65 Morgan is well at the top of MS-65s. But there are some coins far from the top that will not command an MS-65 price—or anything close to it. In fact, there are some MS-65s that many expert numismatists believe should not even be classified as such. Weakly struck MS-65s fall under this classification.

The 1921-S Morgan dollar, graded MS-65 by ANACS (fig. 6-32), is quite a controversial coin. The coin is weakly struck and has been so noted by ANACS on the certificate (no. F-3802-P; L.A.N.; 5-23-85). ANACS believes that strike has no impact on a coin's grade, although many expert numismatists believe that it does. *This coin will not command an MS-65 price.* As of the writing of this book, the *Coin Dealer Newsletter* "ask" price in MS-65 for this date is $1,400, although the MS-64 ask price is $210. The MS-63 ask price is $100, and the MS-60 ask price is $38. **Do not pay an MS-65 price-guide price for a weakly struck coin.**

Many collectors get confused when it becomes necessary to differentiate between weak strike and wear. Weakly struck areas are lustrous and reflect light circularly; wear can be detected because there is an interruption of the original Mint luster, and the light is reflected uniformly. For a thorough explanation of this phenomenon, consult *The Coin Collector's Survival Manual.*

MS-63. MS-63s are identifiable by their facial abrasions, slightly weak strike above the ear, and surfaces that may have been dipped more than once. The 1903-S Morgan dollar, graded MS-63 (fig.

6-33), is one such example. Notice the abrasions above the eye, on the cheek, and to the right of the nose. Furthermore, the hair above the ear is not completely struck.

MS-60. The 1893-O Morgan (fig. 6-34) has one hit on the cheek that is visible to the naked eye. Furthermore, there are scratches and abrasions in the hair. This coin makes it appear as if poor Miss Liberty was the victim of a most unfortunate domestic squabble. Also, the hair above the ear is not fully struck. It should be absolutely clear why this coin grades MS-60.

AU-55. This coin is most deceptive, and it may be difficult from the photograph to tell that it is not Mint State. However, the 1889-CC Morgan dollar (fig. 6-35) grades AU-55. The very lightest of wear is visible on the highest points of the hair, the cotton leaves, and the cap. Furthermore, there is rubbing barely visible in the fields, which can be recognized by the slightly tan coloration.

A Mint State coin reflects light regardless of the angle at which you tilt and rotate it, in much the same way an ocean reflects light: no matter how you look at an ocean, you always see the reflection of light. The About Uncirculated or lightly circulated coin reflects light in the same pattern, *except that at some angles the coin will not reflect light; and the light will be reflected uniformly off of the areas that have been slightly worn.*

EF-40. Some people are so insistent on buying Morgan dollars with no scratches that they end up with heavily circulated coins! The 1893-S (a very rare date) Morgan shown in figure 6-36 looks like what a very inexperienced collector might end up with—in terms of condition—if he or she passed on purchasing nearly perfect examples with some minor flaws. A reputable dealer might never let anything like that happen but one of the very few fly-by-night, unscrupulous dealers might sell this coin as Mint State.

There is wear all over this somewhat dull coin: on the stars, the fields, the cap, the forehead, and especially, the hair above the ear. There are signs of what might be worn-down bagmarks on the cheek.

Morgan Dollar Reverses
As I have stressed repeatedly, toning can cover up a multitude of sins. The MS-63 reverse (of an 1884) shown in figure 6-37 is an even silver-gray and covers up some scattered hit marks in the field. The coin is still a Mint State example, however.

The AU-55 reverse (of an 1882) shown in figure 6-38 is also deeply toned but this reverse is *not* Mint State. The reverse here shows an interruption of the luster. Look at the grayish area in the fields. Notice the white spots on the wing tips. These are areas of wear.

Proof Morgan Dollars

Once again, we are afforded a look at a visual knockout. The 1885 Proof-65 Morgan (fig. 6-39) is spectacularly toned. The autumn-leaves color immediately captures your attention. The original toning coloration is a sight to behold. The bold reds and blues are in their glory. Take note of the lack of hairline scratches on this coin's cheek: the cheek is clean and frosty. (For the purposes of our grading lesson, let us assume that the single unobtrusive nick above the ear was in the die. There is no way of being certain, however, without examining the actual coin.)

The 1895 Morgan (a rare date), graded Proof-63 (fig. 6-40), exhibits hairline scratches. These lines are most noticeable in the left field. The light silver-gray tone does little to obscure these lines, so the grade should be somewhat easy to arrive at. There is also a scratch in front of the eye.

The blocked-off rims and sharp-striking characteristics of these two Proof Morgan dollars can be compared to the business strikes so that you can become more proficient at telling Proof from Prooflike.

Peace and Trade Dollars

Peace dollars free from nicks and scratches are as sought-after as mark-free Morgans. The 1934 Peace dollar, which illustrates the MS-65 grade (fig. 6-41), has a satinlike luster and a solid strike. Do not nitpick. That small spot at 3:00 by the "Y" in Liberty does not lower the grade. The tiny nicks in the hair are minor enough to be tolerated on an MS-65.

The scratches above the eye and on the neck of the 1928 Peace dollar (fig. 6-42), on the other hand, are too severe to be tolerated on an MS-65; and the unattractive, spotty toning lowers the aesthetic appeal. But the major detractions are the scratches. That is why this 1928 dollar is graded MS-63.

Remember, though, that Morgan dollars are not the only dollars that often appear Mint State but are not. The Trade dollar, the United State's only demonetized coin, is sometimes found with deceptive light wear on the highest points. Such coins often closely resemble their Mint State counterparts.

The 1875-S Trade dollar in figure 6-43 is a no-question Mint State example, with delicate honey-golden peripheral toning. Even though toning is evident, wear is not.

But the 1878-S Trade dollar displayed in figure 6-44 is also attractively toned with *much* Mint luster present—but not *all* Mint luster present! This coin is About Uncirculated: *the coin has wear.* Notice the darkened areas, which indicate an interruption of the luster. Most dealers would say this coin has "rub" all over it.

Proof Trade dollars are an extremely popular investment Type coin, but sometimes a coin with serious problems is mistaken for a Proof-65 because of its overwhelmingly beautiful appearance.

First, become familiar with what a real Proof-65 Trade dollar looks like. The 1879 Trade dollar shown in figure 6-45 is an incredible cameo Proof, with deep mirror fields and snow-white devices. It is truly a sight to behold. The slight striking weakness of the head and a few stars does not downgrade this coin.

Now look at the almost equally magnificent 1882 Proof Trade dollar (fig. 6-46). This coin also displays an utterly remarkable cameo contrast, as well as an extraordinarily desirable overall appearance. But wait a second. Do not shell out your money so quickly to pay the Proof-65 price. This coin has three digs in the left obverse field. It could not possibly be a Proof-65; this coin is a Proof-63. You may think that it is a cinch to tell the difference—now that you are an expert. It is not that easy. I have seen some dealers overwhelmed by coins with the type of overall beauty, but detracting marks, that this coin possesses. Some of those dealers even paid the Proof-65 price.

Gold Coins

Gold coins are among the most visually attractive to both collectors and investors, and this universal appeal is reflected in the outstanding performance of high-quality gold coins. But the great demand for high-quality gold has caused those high-grade coins to have correspondingly high price tags attached. As with any other type of United States coin, the primary risk to buyers is not as much of a marketplace risk as it is an acquisition risk.

The following chart was compiled from "bid" levels contained in the September 1985 *Coin Dealer Newsletter Monthly Summary*. Pay particular attention to the difference in price between the Proof-63 and the Proof-65 coins. Often, the visual difference is quite subtle.

PROOF GOLD TYPE COINS

	PROOF-60	PROOF-63	PROOF-65
$1 (type III)	1,750	3,300	9,000
$2½ Liberty	2,100	4,750	10,500
$2½ Indian	2,750	5,750	11,250
$3 Indian	4,400	8,200	19,500
$4 Stella	27,000	36,500	48,000
$5 Liberty	3,000	7,000	13,500
$5 Indian	4,000	8,250	14,750
$10 Liberty	3,600	8,750	18,500
$10 Indian	5,750	11,000	20,000
$20 Liberty	5,500	13,000	27,500
$20 St. Gaudens	11,000	18,250	31,500

Even if you do not collect Proof gold (or have never even seen a Proof gold piece), pay careful attention to the price differences in this chart. They have applications to your area of collecting or investing, whether that area be assembling a set of circulated Lincoln cents or putting together a set of Proof Liberty Seated quarters.

Quarter-Eagles

The differences in grade among Proof gold coins, as well as among business-strike gold coins, can sometimes be difficult to detect. Let us take a look at an 1870 Proof-65 quarter-eagle gold piece (fig. 6-47). There is little to talk about except the coin's beauty. The cameo contrast helps make this example particularly alluring.

Now let us take a look at an 1895 Proof quarter-eagle (fig. 6-48). This coin has that magically appealing look. But wait! It is not a Proof-65; there are digs out in the right field, as indicated by the arrow.

The 1892 Proof-60 quarter-eagle (fig. 6-49) has digs, as well as various other detracting marks, and lacks that magical look that should be apparent to you if you compare it with the coin in figure 6-48. This coin might even have been dipped.

Just because a coin is a Proof does not mean that it cannot have wear on its high points. The 1891 quarter-eagle, graded Proof-55 (fig. 6-50), is an "impaired Proof." Notice the dullness of the high points and the fields. If you were actually to examine this coin, you might see reflective surfaces interrupted by a graininess, which you should be able to identify as wear.

Eagles

Every collector to whom I have shown the photograph of the 1801 eagle (fig. 6-51) comments on what a beautiful coin it is. "But it grades AU-55," I always say. "Who cares, it's a nice coin anyway," the collector always replies. This proves a point: a coin does not always have to be MS-65 or even MS-60 to be attractive both as a collectible and as an investment. If you like the coin, terrific. But do not buy it at a Mint State price if it is not Mint State.

The 1801 eagle had a lighter color on the highest points, as indicated by the multiple arrows. Early gold is difficult to obtain in no-question Mint State condition, although a great demand exists for it. Sellers sometimes succumb to buyer pressures and push the grade description of a nice AU-55, such as this one, to Mint State.

But those gold coins that most often sell for MS-65 prices, but are not MS-65s, are what the marketplace calls "MS-64s." Such a coin will usually have a near-perfect cheek but have a detracting gouge or scratch in the field. The 1901-S eagle, graded MS-64 (fig. 6-52), is one such coin.

That MS-64 eagle is temptingly close to MS-65, but there is a scratch in the left field, as indicated by the arrow, which prevents the full 65 designation. There are also some other very minor detractions, which in-and-of themselves would not cause a downgrading to 64.

The 1893 eagle in MS-60 (fig. 6-53) has detractions visible to the naked eye. A scruffy-looking coin such as this one cannot qualify for any grade higher than MS-60. However, there is no wear, so the coin is still in the Mint State category, unlike the 1853-O Eagle (fig. 6-54), which is no better than About Uncirculated.

Double-Eagles

The grading of double-eagle gold pieces is similar to the grading of silver dollars. Both silver dollars and double-eagles are large coins and are apt to be heavily marked, nicked, and gouged. When a double-eagle business strike surfaces that is mark-free, it is often sold immediately.

The 1884-CC double-eagle, graded MS-64 (fig. 6-55), is close to 65, but there are rim problems and a light facial scrape. With a few less marks, this coin would grade MS-65. The real Mint State example needs to display full luster, as this specimen does.

The About Uncirculated-55 double-eagle (fig. 6-56) is lackluster and, once again, has rub visible all over it. The original luster can be seen as a ring around the stars, the date, and the portrait.

A Mint State coin must have luster. The 1876-CC double-eagle in figure 6-57 has uniform wear all over it but still might have some luster. Pay particular attention to the lack of detail in the portrait.

There is no rule that says a grading chapter must be a textbook explanation of what to look for, with no incentive to collect. The 1890 Proof-65 double-eagle (fig. 6-58) proves this. You probably are not as interested in knowing that this coin grades Proof-65 as you are in just looking at the coin and appreciating its beauty! The cameo contrast is intense, and the overall appearance is splendid. Just looking at a coin of this magnitude should convert some un-knowledgeable investors into people who, at the very least, appreciate the artistic aspect of numismatics.

The 1899 Proof-64 double-eagle (fig. 6-59) is very nearly as nice as the 1890 Proof-65, except that this coin has some facial scratches that are difficult to see in the photograph but are visible, nevertheless. Furthermore, there are some light hairline scratches on the coin itself that are not too visible from the picture, but which I saw while borrowing the actual coin from a dealer who paid $17,600 for it at the 1985 A.N.A. auction in Baltimore.

There are Proof twenties that are obvious 63s, as the 1903

Proof-63 (fig. 6-60) demonstrates. This coin has spots that are visible to the naked eye and that are quite detracting. These spots apparently penetrate the surface and are more than mere light toning areas.

Proof twenties are sometimes found impaired, and you should beware of such coins. The 1906 Proof twenty shown in figure 6-61 displays signs of contact. Many numismatic experts might even grade this coin Proof-55. But whether it is graded Proof-55 or Proof-60 is not as important as your realizing that it is not a Proof-65. There is also a rim nick at 2:00.

MS-65 Saint-Gaudens double-eagles have been high-performance coins, and their size makes them appealing to investors. But solid MS-65s are few and far between. The market has remained hot in this area with almost no letup. Consequently, marketplace grading standards have loosened considerably. As of the writing of this book, I have not seen a true MS-67 Saint since 1980.

The 1908 Saint-Gaudens double-eagle without motto (fig. 6-62) has been graded MS-65 by ANACS in 1985. The coin has a beautiful satiny luster and has virtually no marks of consequence. (Again, do not nitpick. Those toning spots in the right obverse field do not affect the grade.) This particular date, however, tends to have a softer look than other dates in this series; do not expect every MS-65 to have this soft look.

MS-63s are easy to identify: they have marks; they are scuffy. But if there are very few MS-65s around, a good number of MS-64s will trade as MS-65s. For example, the 1909-D grades MS-63 (fig. 6-63)—it has scattered marks. Compare it with the 1908 MS-65, and you will see the difference. Pay attention to the difference in luster quality and the MS-65's absence of marks. There is no wear on the high points of the 1909-D, but there are marks.

AU-55 Saints are commonplace and deceptive. Most have much original luster with only the faintest trace of wear on the high points. The 1925-S "slider" (a coin with slide marks at its highest points, indicating wear) Saint (fig. 6-64) could easily pass for MS-63. There is wear on the right breast and right knee (the left breast and left knee to Miss Liberty), as indicated by the arrows.

A SURVEY OF MAJOR COIN-GRADING SERVICES

Grading rare coins is a multimillion-dollar business. Pristine Mint-State coins—those in the highest grades (or levels of preservation)—have soared in value, but small degrees of difference in the quality of a coin can raise or lower its value by many thousands of dollars. As a consequence, accurate grading has become more vital than ever in the marketplace, and demand for expertise has spawned a growing number of coin-grading services to render informed judgments on the subject.

The volume of coins being graded is evident from the fact that in December 1988, shortly before its third anniversary, the Professional Coin Grading Service (PCGS) graded its one-millionth coin. By mid-1989, PCGS—the largest of the services—had graded more than 1,250,000 coins. Its leading rival, the Numismatic Guaranty Corporation of America (NGC), had graded some 300,000 coins by that point—and NGC wasn't yet two years old at the time.

A comprehensive study of every grading service would be impractical, if not impossible, within the scope of this book. The field has gotten crowded, and even as this is written, new firms are springing up. **Consumers are warned to only purchase coins graded by grading services whose prices are listed in *The Certified Coin Dealer Newsletter* (a weekly pricing guide of the certified market). The potential for abuse by unproven grading services is significant.**

Four grading services stand above the rest in terms of market acceptance, and by analyzing these we can draw some general conclusions about the role being played by the services as a whole—and how they can be used to greatest advantage.

The four most widely accepted grading services are:

American Numismatic Association Certification Service (ANACS)
818 North Cascade Avenue
Colorado Springs, CO 80903

Of the four leading services, ANACS is the oldest. It started grading coins in 1979, and it dates back even further—to 1972—as a coin authentication service (one that passes judgment on whether a coin is genuine). It was formed under the auspices of the American Numismatic Association (ANA), the nation's largest organized coin club.

The ANA grading system employs a numerical scale from 1 to 70, with 70 denoting perfection—an absolutely flawless coin. Under this system, 11 different grades ranging from 60 to 70 fall within the Mint-State spectrum. The other major services use the same numerical framework, but each has its own interpretation of the standards—its own criteria for coins of a given grade. Thus, a coin graded Mint State-65 (MS-65) by ANACS might be viewed as MS-64 or MS-66 by one of the other services.

In 1989, ANACS introduced a special plastic holder called the "Cache." Customers can have an ANACS-certified coin sealed in one of these holders if they wish. The service also offers photo certification without encapsulation. Some collectors favor this approach, since they then retain full, direct access to their coins. However, only coins in sealed plastic holders—also known as "slabs"—enjoy complete liquidity and are bought and sold routinely on a sight-unseen basis like commodities. ANACS's slabbed coins are graded with an overall marketplace grade (e.g., MS-65); and ANACS's photo-certificate coins are graded on the obverse and reverse (e.g., MS-65/64).

Because it is an arm of the national coin club, ANACS is widely perceived as more collector-oriented than competing grading services. Its simon-pure image was reinforced for years by the fact that it had no dealer affiliation. But this was a double-edged sword: While making ANACS grading more palatable to some, its "amateur" status also stirred concern about the quality of the grading. The ANA sought to counter this in 1989 by seeking the grading and consulting services of a national organization composed of several hundred coin dealers.

Coins can be submitted to ANACS by individual collectors or investors. But slab submissions must be made through ANACS's authorized dealer network. By contrast, some services accept submissions only from dealer members. At present, ANACS offers three basic services: photo certification for $23, encapsulation in the Cache, also for $23, and photo certification plus encapsulation for $30. Turnaround time is 60 working days. Five-day express service is available; the fee for this is $40. For $65, the coin is graded within 2 days. One-day express encapsulation service costs $125.

Numismatic Certification Institute (NCI)
311 Market Street
Dallas, TX 75202

NCI is an affiliate of Heritage Capital Corporation, the Dallas conglomerate which touts itself as the world's largest coin dealer. The grading service was founded in 1984.

James L. Halperin, co-chairman of the board of Heritage, has acknowledged that NCI's grading standards are less conservative than those of the other leading services. He says they are from 1 to $1\frac{1}{2}$ points looser than the standards of PCGS, NGC, and ANACS.

This presents no problem for those who buy and sell NCI-graded coins—as long as they do so at prices that correspond to NCI grading. A coin graded MS-65 by NCI isn't worth as much as coins of the same type graded MS-65 by PCGS, NGC, or ANACS. Having been graded more strictly, those are better coins. But the NCI coin may still be a good buy if purchased at a price accurately reflecting its somewhat lower quality.

Problems do arise with NCI coins on occasion, but not because of the grading itself. Rather, they occur because of misuse of NCI coins by unscrupulous telemarketers. These fast-talking telephone sales-men sell NCI-graded coins to unwary customers—buyers unfamiliar with the coin market—at prices corresponding to the current market value of PCGS, NGC, or ANACS coins of the same grade. Often, those may be hundreds or even thousands of dollars higher than the value of the NCI coins.

Prices for certified coins from all the major services are listed each week in the *Certified Coin Dealer Newsletter,* a publication com-monly referred to as the "Blue Sheet" because of its color. In buying or selling any certified coin, be absolutely certain to check the Blue Sheet price not only for the grade in question but also for the service that graded the coin.

Because NCI is owned by a coin company, concerns were voiced initially that the company would use it to gain a competitive edge by grading its own coins optimistically. Five years' experience suggests that these fears were unfounded. Heritage has made a good-faith effort to segregate NCI from its retail coin business—and, for the most part, has succeeded.

Like ANACS, NCI assigns split grades when it judges one side of a coin to be better than the other. Also like ANACS, it accepts submissions from individual collectors and investors. In practice, however, about 80 percent of the coins submitted to it for grading come from dealers. NCI has a slabbing "option," but, unlike ANACS, the slab grade is the same as the certificate grade.

For regular service, NCI charges $29 apiece for the first 20 coins and $24 apiece for any coins above that amount. Turnaround time is 15 business days. Express service takes 7 business days and costs $40 per coin. Walk-through service takes 2 business days and costs $75.

NCI furnishes a photo certificate with every coin it grades. For $6 more, NCI's slab option may be exercised.

Professional Coin Grading Service (PCGS)
P.O. Box 9458
Newport Beach, CA 92658

The founding of PCGS in February 1986 triggered what has been called a "grading revolution." Almost overnight, the company revo-lutionized the way rare coins are graded and the way they are bought and sold.

For one thing, it pioneered the use of all 11 Mint-State numerical grades from 60 to 70. Prior to that time, almost every Mint-State coin was assigned one of four basic grades: MS-60, 63, 65, or 67.

Some dealers also recognized the intermediate grade of MS-64, but virtually no one was using the whole spectrum. Conventional wisdom decreed that grading could never be precise enough to justify so fine-tuned an approach.

David Hall, the founder and president of PCGS, maintained that precision grading was indeed possible through a process of consensus involving expert graders. Under the system devised by Hall, three such experts examine and grade each coin and their judgments are then reviewed by a fourth and final grader known as the "finalizer." If all four agree, the grade they have decided upon is assigned. If there is disagreement, other graders are consulted until at length consensus is achieved. At PCGS, all graders are full-time professional numismatists.

Of all the innovations introduced by PCGS, none was more important than the use of a hard plastic holder—or "slab"—to house each coin after grading. This holder protects the coin, but its most important function is really to protect the company's guarantee. Sonically sealed in each "slab," along with the coin, is a small tab denoting the type and date of the coin and the grade it was assigned by PCGS. A code number also appears. PCGS guarantees the accuracy of its grading: If a coin is resubmitted (in its original holder) and receives a lower grade, the company will pay the owner the difference in market value between the two grades.

PCGS has established a network of member dealers who are obligated to purchase PCGS-graded coins sight-unseen at the grade assigned by the service. Along with the plastic holder, this has been the key to the marketplace acceptance of its coins. As of mid-1989, there were nearly 400 PCGS dealer members, including most of the industry's biggest and most important dealers. The liquidity of PCGS coins is further enhanced by the fact that they change hands routinely on the American Numismatic Exchange (ANE), a national coin-trading network.

Coins can be submitted to PCGS only through member dealers. The company charges $26 per coin for regular service. Estimated turnaround time is 60 to 80 working days. Other options include express service—with a guaranteed return within 12 working days—for $59 and super-express service in 72 hours or less for $85. Walk-through service is available, but as of May 1989 the price for this was $300 and reportedly headed higher. This special service is offered by appointment only.

Numismatic Guaranty Corporation of America (NGC)
P.O. Box 1776
Parsippany, NJ 07054

The founder of NGC, John Albanese, was among the small group of professional numismatists who helped David Hall establish PCGS. Albanese embraced most of the grading reforms introduced by PCGS, but felt that there could never be truly objective grading unless the company's principals divorced themselves from buying and selling coins. Hall and other principals of PCGS have continued to deal in coins, but Albanese decided to practice what he preached: He gave up his job as buyer for a major coin firm and founded NGC.

NGC began grading coins in August 1987 and soon established itself as PCGS's leading competitor. In many ways, its operations parallel those of PCGS: It grades coins by consensus, it encapsulates each coin in a hard plastic holder, it maintains a dealer network, and it guarantees its grading. But while NGC employs professional numismatists—coin dealers—to do its preliminary grading, finalizers must be full-time employees of the company and cannot engage in buying and selling coins. Albanese views this "arm's-length" approach to grading as the key to NGC's current success and long-term stability.

NGC is known for the strictness and consistency of its grading. In a number of areas, it has graded coins more strictly than other leading services—including PCGS. Often, NGC coins bring prices that are equal to, or higher than, those of comparably graded coins of the same type from other grading services.

NGC has gained a reputation, as well, for consumer advocacy. It has taken a firm stand, for example, against the certification of most late-date U.S. coins, contending that certain dealers are selling such coins for grossly inflated prices—prices unwarranted by the ample supply of these coins—just because they carry high Mint-State grades from a grading service.

Regular service at NGC costs $23 and involves a turnaround time of 10 to 12 weeks. Express service costs $40 and provides a return within 6 working days. Overnight grading ("dispatch") costs $75.

None of the leading services will encapsulate problem coins—those that have been cleaned, artificially toned, damaged by chemicals such as polyvinyl chloride (PVC), or have other significant flaws. Such coins would jeopardize the integrity and liquidity of sight-unseen trading.

The Detection of Altered and Counterfeit Coins

Rapidly advancing technology has given the criminal element the means to create increasingly deceptive altered and counterfeit coins. But that technology is also used in the *detection* of inauthentic coins. Thus, counterfeit and altered coins pose little more of a problem today than they did two years ago or twenty years ago.

Counterfeit and altered coins are not this industry's primary problem. The Hobby Protection Act of 1974 makes the selling of counterfeit or altered coins a *punishable offense.* And a number of dealers offer guarantees which state that their firms will pay you a certain compounded percentage per year if any coins they sell are later proven to be altered or counterfeit. However, a basic knowledge of the various types of counterfeit and altered coins is helpful. And the use of a high-power magnifying glass or stereomicroscope to assist in detecting altered and counterfeit coins will not hurt.

The American Numismatic Association Certification Service, the International Numismatic Society Authentication Bureau, and other opinion-rendering services have played a large role in sounding alerts when they need to be sounded.

An editorial in *Coin World* about the skills of ANACS in detecting a particularly deceptive and authentic-looking counterfeit and sounding the alert points out ANACS's authentication abilities, keen judgment, and intuitive feel. It reads, in part:

> Every red-blooded collector and dealer knows about that "sheer instinct" feeling, but it took the records ANACS has constructed, its micro-photographic files, and its experience factor on the part of its staff to

declare without a doubt the counterfeit has infiltrated the mainstream of the hobby. But not for long now, thanks to ANACS. The hobby warning it has sounded ought to be a lesson of equal proportion to the coin fakers who try to refine their evil science to the ultimate. Counterfeiters can't win these days with such resources for detection now in place at ANA headquarters in Colorado Springs. We congratulate and thank ANACS, the ANA dealers and collectors who have helped, not only with this particular counterfeit exposé, but with contributions to the ANA reference cabinet of good and bad coins. It is a well-known fact counterfeiters have no principles, but they have never had to reckon with the scientific detection now in place at ANACS or its power to sound the alert. They may have met their Waterloo.

ALTERED COINS

Altered coins are found in all sizes, shapes, and varieties. An altered coin is not a coin that is fake but a real coin that has been doctored to look like another coin. For example, if a coin is manufactured by the Mint with a Mint-mark and has that mark removed by someone after the coin has been manufactured, it is considered to be altered.

The bad news is that altered coins are found of virtually every scarce date and variety. The good news is that these coins are not always very difficult to detect. Many times, detecting an altered coin requires merely a keen eye and common sense.

The "1904-S" Morgan dollar illustrated (figs. 7-1, 7-2, and 7-3) is not a 1904-S. It is a combination of two altered coins: a 1904-P with a hollowed-out or honed reverse, but with the left rim and edge intact where the rim meets the denticles; and an S-reverse from another Morgan dollar. The two pieces were placed together like a puzzle.

This particular coin is a well-made example, but it can still be detected, as you can see from careful inspection of the rim (fig. 7-3). The telltale seam is between the denticles and rim, where the arrow is pointing. ANACS authenticator/grader Pedro Collazo-Oliver estimates that it took about an hour for these two coins to be altered and combined into one deceptive specimen.

This type of alteration can be found in many kinds of coins in which a small alteration can mean a substantial difference in price. Collazo-Oliver says that he has seen examples of 1909-S V.D.B. Lincoln cents and Morgan dollars of the dates and Mint-marks 1889-CC and 1893-S.

Coins are also altered by Mint-marks simply being removed or added (or carved out).

Fig. 7-1. "1904-S" Morgan dollar obverse. This is a genuine coin whose reverse was hollowed out. (Photo courtesy Pedro Collazo-Oliver)

Fig. 7-2. "S" reverse. This is the reverse of the 1904 with the entire "S" reverse added. The reverse was placed into the hollowed-out 1904 obverse like a puzzle. (Photo courtesy Pedro Collazo-Oliver)

Fig. 7-3. The telltale seam between the denticles and the rim is clearly visible in this blow-up of an assembled Morgan dollar. (Photo courtesy Pedro Collazo-Oliver)

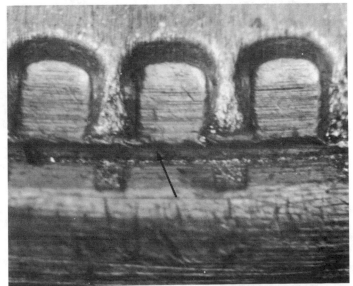

GRADE ALTERATIONS

Coins can be altered in other ways so that their grades appear higher. A wire brush and a chemical can be used to upgrade a coin artificially. This is called "whizzing." These coins are identified by their lack of detail and their granular surfaces.

A coin can be acid treated so that the devices appear frosted, or a scratch can be masked. These coins can be identified by the spillover from the devices into the field. Use a high-power magnifying glass to identify these coins.

Be particularly careful of details that have been reëngraved. These are often easily detected. The reverse of the Mercury dime in figure 7-4 is one such example. A sharp-bladed knife was probably used to make the bands appear split, as indicated by the arrow.

CAST COUNTERFEITS

Cast counterfeits can often be detected by their characteristically grainy, porous surfaces. Many such coins are crude indeed, for they were manufactured many years ago to be passed off as pocket change.

Fig. 7-4. The crudely altered upper bands (not even the primary place of examination for full split-band determination!) are clearly visible upon close inspection. (Photo courtesy Pedro Collazo-Oliver)

The cast counterfeit is, technically, a copy of a copy. These types of counterfeits are sometimes oily or greasy and usually lack a good deal of detail.

DIE-STRUCK COUNTERFEITS

The die-struck counterfeit, which simulates the Mint process, is the most difficult to detect; the *Coin World* editorial excerpted earlier refers to such a counterfeit.

Die-struck counterfeits can often be detected only by knowing what the counterfeit die looks like, and there are many. It is beyond the scope of this, or any other, book to list all of these varieties.

The beautiful 1903 Liberty head double-eagle obverse displayed in figure 7-5 is a die-struck counterfeit. However, the best way to determine that it is a fake is by knowing the die varieties of the counterfeit: roughness above the eye and doubling of the stars, as indicated by the arrows.

The 1878 $3 gold counterfeit (figs. 7-6, 7-7, and 7-8) is another such example. A cursory glance might not reveal that it is inauthentic but there are numerous die characteristics that allow the experienced numismatist to detect its lack of authenticity.

There is a die scratch in between the "I" and "B" of Liberty (figs. 7-6 and 7-8), as indicated by the arrows. There are die scratches beneath the denticles and above the "A" of America. On the reverse, there is a small piece of metal on the top denticle, and there is a rippled appearance to the area just beneath the bow, as indicated by the arrow. Furthermore, there are small spikes between the denticles.

A VIDEO GUIDE TO COUNTERFEITS

More information about the detection of altered and counterfeit coins can be obtained from the organizations mentioned at the end of chapter 6.

However, interested individuals may purchase a videotape (available in either Beta or VHS) that takes the viewer on an optical journey through the intricacies of the detection of inauthentic coins. The tape, endorsed by the American Numismatic Association, is titled, *Coins: Genuine, Counterfeit, Altered.*

It is available from Education Video, Inc. (31800 Plymouth Road, Livonia, MI 48150) for $59.95, plus $2.00 for U.P.S. and handling charges. Michigan residents should add the appropriate sales tax.

Fig. 7-5. Counterfeit 1903 double-eagle. This die-struck counterfeit is quite deceiving. However, it is identifiable if you are familiar with the characteristic die marks visible on the counterfeit, as indicated by the arrows. (Photo courtesy Pedro Collazo-Oliver)

Fig. 7-6. Counterfeit 1878 three-dollar gold piece. This die-struck counterfeit can be detected through its die characteristics, such as the die scratch between the "I" and "B" of LIBERTY. (Photo courtesy Pedro Collazo-Oliver)

Fig. 7-7. Reverse of the 1878 three-dollar gold piece. The die scratches are another indicator that this coin is counterfeit. (Photo courtesy Pedro Collazo-Oliver)

Fig. 7-8. This is a blow-up of the die scratch between the "I" and "B" of LIBERTY. (Photo courtesy Pedro Collazo-Oliver)

Estate Planning, Government Regulation, and Taxes

Anybody who thinks that estate planning and careful use of gift-giving to the next generation isn't necessary should have a one-sentence will that reads: "I leave my assets to the United States of America."

—*David L. Ganz*
Numismatic lawyer

Stories of spectacular profits from rare coin investment abound. One often-told story concerns the sale of the collection of New York lawyer Harold Bareford. This shrewd attorney paid $13,832 for a collection of gold coins that realized $1,207,215 in December 1978—even before the great 1979–80 boom! Some of the 242 coins were held for over thirty years.

What few people mention when discussing Bareford, however, was that his collection was sold *after* his death. Bareford's heirs were lucky. Here was a man who carefully selected coins for his collection as a means of both recreation and capital preservation. And the collection was disposed of *profitably*.

But many people do not bother planning for the passing on of assets to the next generation. Often, coins will be sold for a fraction of their real value to an *unscrupulous* dealer. Or they just might disappear from an unsecured drawer—without a trace. In the case of a person without a will, assets might be divided among heirs in a way that is unacceptable to many of them.

It is your responsibility to educate your heirs as to how the coin market operates and how your coins should be disposed of. Some auction companies recommend a codicil to your will which indicates that a particular auction firm should handle the liquidation. However, this is not binding.

To plan your estate properly, the intricacies of your personal finances should be discussed with a lawyer who is expert in trusts and estates. Every situation is different, and yours might require immediate liquidation of some coins or the giving of others as gifts. Perhaps you may want to create a trust. In any case, you do need to plan. A detailed discussion of these matters is beyond the scope of this book.

Your goal should not be one of short-term trading like stocks. Coins are a wealth asset, and there is no one time that you should sell all of your coins and enter into another investment. Coins move in cycles. If some of your coins have increased in price greatly in a short period of time, it might be prudent to sell them and buy other coins. Or you might want to trade some coins that have not moved in a long time for others that you think are about to make a move. But, in general, coins should be used to preserve your capital over the long term and to transfer to the next generation.

HOW TO SECURE A NUMISMATIC COLLATERAL LOAN

Discussions about rare coins gaining credibility as a traditional investment medium are never concluded until someone poses the question of whether coins can be used as collateral. Conventional financial, legal, and accounting wisdom says that an asset that can be easily converted into collateral is an asset with universally recognized and real—not arbitrary—value.

Yes, coins can—and often are—used for collateral loans, but the use of the collateral loan does far more to promote the liquidity of the coin market as a whole and give the appearance of a viable investment market than it does to help the borrower. It is great that this type of loan is available, but its uses are limited.

It is one thing to get a loan on a house if you live there or to get a loan on a car that serves as your primary means of transport. But coins should be used as a *supplement* to traditional modes of investment. You should not need to get a loan to buy coins. The money you use to buy coins with should constitute a small part of your net worth and be disposable income. In other words, if you need a loan to buy the coins, you should not buy them at all. Furthermore, the rate on coin loans is often *3 percent* above the usual rate.

Nevertheless, there are some useful purposes for the numismatic loan; such as when you get yourself into a financial bind and have no source of income, but do not want to sell your coins because the market is too depressed. Dealers, too, find useful purposes for this type of loan.

Joel Gabrelow, formerly senior vice-president of the now-defunct Valley State Bank writing in the October 1984 *Coin Dealer Newsletter Monthly Summary,* offers the following guidelines for securing a numismatic collateral loan. (In a telephone interview, Gabrelow indicated that these guidelines have remained stable over the past few years and that he sees no reason for them to change in the near future.) Gabrelow writes, in part:

• Contact the lending officer in the appropriate department (asset lending is often the name of choice). A telephone call is best, as the bank officer can usually determine if the collateral meets the bank's requirement. In the case of precious metals, the banker can usually provide an exact loan amount.
• If you do not meet the requirements, you will probably be requested to ship the collateral directly to the bank. Rare coins always take an extra day or two, usually because the bank must evaluate them before sending loan documents.
• You will receive loan documents and will be requested to sign and return them along with a short financial statement form.
• Once the bank has received the collateral and signed the documents, it can fund your loan.
• Loans can be funded in the form of a cashier's check or bank wire and sent anywhere in the world.
• Loans are generally written up for a 180-day term. Shorter- or longer-term loans can be written, depending on the size and liquidity of the collateral.
• Interest rates can range from as low as "prime" to prime plus X. Origination fees range from 2 percent to 3 percent of the loan amount. Fees can be higher or lower depending upon the size of the loan.
• Rare coins held as collateral will be valued at the borrower's estimates for insurance purposes if the values are reasonable and are commensurate with the market. Precious metals are insured on a replacement basis, so value on a particular day is not a factor.
• When paying off a loan, the bank requires good funds before releasing the collateral.
• If the market should decline to the extent that it affects the value of the collateral being held at the bank, the bank will request that the borrower reduce the principal of his or her loan, or he or she may add collateral in an amount of the demand.

- In the unlikely event of a borrower unable to meet his or her obligations in a timely manner, his or her coins will be liquidated to retire his or her obligation to the bank. Any excess will be forwarded to the borrower, if any should exist.

A sample of what a numismatic collateral receipt looks like is provided in figure 8-1. There are columns for denominations, dates, and Mint-marks.

Institutions that offer collateral coin loans have done a great deal to help show the investment community that coins are recognized stores of value. The very fact that numismatic collateral loans exist helps your coin investments appreciate in value.

COINS AND TAXES

Not everyone who invests in rare coins becomes a coin collector. But all prudent investors keep close tabs on at least one collector: the one who collects their taxes.

Like every form of investment, rare coins have tax implications. Knowing what they are—and how to deal with them properly (and sometimes creatively)—can save you a pretty penny.

Gains and Losses

"Gold, silver, stamps, coins, gems, etc., are capital assets except when they are held for sale by a dealer. Any gain or loss you have from their sale or trade generally is a capital gain or loss."

So said the Internal Revenue Service in *Your Federal Income Tax,* a publication issued for individuals' use in preparing 1988 federal income tax returns. The statement seems straightforward, but in practice there can be some tricky twists and turns.

The Tax Reform Act of 1986 eliminated one of the most important tax benefits previously available to rare-coin investors: the capital-gains treatment of the profits they derive from selling their coins advantageously. Capital gains are now taxed at the same rate as ordinary income—up to 33 percent for the typical coin investor, who tends to be a higher-income individual. Previously, the tax rate had been only 20 percent on long-term capital gains, including the gains from selling collectibles held for more than six months.

Owners of rare coins also lost a series of other deductions which, while possibly modest in their own right, could be quite substantial in the aggregate. Effective January 1, 1987, they could no longer claim deductions for:

- Sales taxes on hobby-related purchases.
- Rental fees for safe deposit boxes where they store all or part of their coins.
- The cost of books or periodicals purchased in conjunction with collectibles being treated as investments.

In addition, the new law provided for a phase-out of tax deductibility for interest paid on most consumer loans, including credit-card accounts, eliminating the benefit entirely after 1990. This makes it less attractive for collectors and investors to go into debt to finance new acquisitions.

The impact of the tax law on coin-related transactions was not entirely negative. Investors may actually be better off than before, for example, in cases where they sell coins at a loss. Under the 1986 law, 100 percent of net capital losses (the amount by which capital losses exceed capital gains) may now be deducted against ordinary income up to a maximum of $3,000. Previously, the limit was the same, but while short-term capital losses could be deducted in full up to $3,000, only 50 percent of long-term capital losses (those involving assets held for more than six months) could be deducted, and typically rare coins are long-term assets. In effect, the new law has eliminated the distinction between short-term and long-term capital gains and losses. Myron S. Lubell, a well-known tax expert and columnist, has pointed out that "this subtle change often may have the effect of doubling the loss limit." According to Lubell, "Any excess loss can be carried over indefinitely until used up."

Like-Kind Exchanges

One way to avoid the new, higher tax rate on gains from the sale of coins is to trade them instead for other coins. The IRS permits deferral of taxes in such instances—but only if the trade is a "like-kind" exchange.

This can be an extremely beneficial maneuver. By using it, you can realize a profit on a coin without paying tax for years on your gain from the transaction. (Your profit comes from the fact that your new coin is worth more than the price you paid originally for the first coin.) Keep in mind, however, that the coins involved in the trade must qualify as "like-kind" in the eyes of the IRS.

The IRS has interpreted "like-kind" as referring to the nature of property, not the condition. Thus, it would probably disallow like-kind treatment for a trade involving a Canadian Maple Leaf gold bullion coin and a rare United States copper coin. On the other hand, it might well accept the exchange of one copper coin graded MS-65 for another graded only Fine-12.

"A trade means an actual barter of the coins," says D. Larry Crumbley, Shelton taxation professor at Texas A & M University and author of numerous books and articles on tax matters. "You cannot merely sell your coins and reinvest the proceeds into more coins."

According to Crumbley, "Like-kind exchanges might involve trading numismatic coins for numismatic coins or trading bullion coins for bullion coins. But like-kind exchanges would not include trading bullion coins for numismatic coins or numismatic coins for bullion coins."

The IRS will collect taxes eventually on the gain in value, when you elect to sell the coin or coins obtained in such a trade. For tax purposes, Crumbley says, the gain is determined by how much you paid for the first item involved in an exchange (or a series of exchanges). "The basis for each coin is transferred to the items for which it is traded," he says.

In effect, like-kind exchanges enable you to postpone your tax obligation—perhaps until a time when you are in a lower tax bracket or otherwise better able to afford it. Be cautious, however, in using this device. I strongly recommend that you seek the counsel of a competent tax advisor before entering into a trade you plan to claim as a like-kind exchange.

Reporting Requirements

The purchase or sale of coins may be subject to one of several IRS reporting requirements.

One of these pertains to cash transactions. The IRS requires that:

> Each person engaged in a trade or business who, in the course of such trade or business, receives more than $10,000 in cash in one transaction (or two or more related transactions) must file Form 8300. For example, multiple receipts of cash from any person which in any one day total more than $10,000 should be treated as a single receipt (and therefore reportable).

In 1988, Congress passed legislation authorizing the Secretary of the Treasury to reduce the cash threshold, at his discretion, to any figure he chooses below $10,000 per transaction. As of this writing, the Secretary had not exercised this prerogative. The intent of the legislation was to give law-enforcement agencies a stronger legal weapon in their war against drug traffickers. Critics have argued, however, that lowering the threshold would simply create a blizzard of unprocessable paperwork.

Your rare-coin purchases may be private; indeed, rare coins' appeal is enhanced by the fact that being small and portable, they can be bought, sold and stored inconspicuously. But remember that under certain circumstances, cash transactions are reportable to the government.

Yet another reporting requirement was added to the IRS code by the Tax Equity and Fiscal Responsibility Act (TEFRA). This section (Section 6045) requires bullion dealers to file a report (Form 1099-B) on each transaction covered by Commodity Futures Trading Commission (CFTC) contracts. The IRS promulgated regulations spelling out details of this requirement in 1983, but rescinded them soon afterward when they stirred considerable controversy. It then published proposed new regulations in 1984, but delayed formal adoption of these guidelines. As of early June 1989, the new regulations still had not been formalized.

This reporting requirement appears to pertain to most bullion transactions, including those involving the sale or purchase of bullion-type coins (those whose price is based on the value of the metal they contain). However, in the absence of official IRS guidelines, the rule has been subject to widely varying interpretations. It is generally agreed that the IRS need not be notified if the premium on a coin exceeds 15 percent of the coin's bullion value.

Because of the reporting requirement, many investors have turned from buying gold and other precious metals to buying numismatic coins—rare coins—instead. Since these carry premiums well above 15 percent of their intrinsic value, they are not subject to the reporting rule and therefore afford significantly greater privacy.

Coins in Retirement Plans

Section 314-b of the Economic Recovery Act of 1981 effectively barred coins from self-directed Keogh plans and Individual Retirement Accounts. Though it didn't specifically ban them, it removed the tax incentives that made their inclusion financially attractive.

The Tax Reform Act of 1986 created an important exception. It permitted IRAs to invest in American Eagle gold and silver bullion coins. Presumably, this was done to encourage the sale of these coins, produced by the United States Mint, which made their first appearance around the time the tax law was enacted. The law did not relax the restriction on other coins, nor did it permit the inclusion of American Eagles in Keogh plans or corporate retirement plans.

This is a volatile area that is expected to change; please keep abreast of events. The Industry Council for Tangible Assets (ICTA, 214 Massachusetts Avenue, N.E., Suite 560, Washington, DC 20002) is a lobby organization that is trying to help coins retain favorable tax treatment.

COLLATERAL RECEIPT
NON NEGOTIABLE
NON FUNGIBLE

PAGE _____ OF _____

19 _____

Deposited by _____

QUANTITY	DENOM	DATE	MM	TYPE	GRADE	OTHER

Rec'd From: _____ Date: _____

Sent to: _____ Date: _____

Replaces C/R # _____ Date: _____

Replaced by C/R # _____ Date: _____

Closed by: _____ Date: _____

Note # _____

Account # _____

INSTRUCTIONS FOR RETURN OF COLLATERAL
AND DISPOSITION:

_____

_____

_____

_____

By: _____

By: _____ OFFICE NO. _____

NON-FUNGIBLE
SEGREGATED STORAGE

Fig. 8-1. Numismatic collateral receipt. This is what a receipt for numismatic material cn which a collateral loan is based looks like. (Courtesy Valley State Bank)

119

Lately, some publicity has been given to coins being allowed in managed retirement plans. This is legal but not practical. The manager would hold a fiduciary responsibility to place only prudent investments in the retirement plan. In other words, if the coin investment lost money, the manager who allowed the coins in the plan might be held personally liable.

HOW TO KEEP RECORDS

Your records should be kept so that someone who knows nothing about coins would be able to understand them. Carefully record the name of the coin, a description of the coin, as well as the source from which you purchased it and the amount paid. The date of purchase should also be included. If you have sold a coin, but still have it listed in your log, note the date on which it was sold as well as the price it was sold for.

Keep all receipts, and prepare a letter to your heirs indicating how you would like the coins to be disposed of. Keep this letter in a safe-deposit box or other secure place.

In addition, keep a log of up-to-date value listings of your numismatic holdings.

HOW TO DETERMINE WHETHER YOU ARE A COLLECTOR OR A DEALER

It is by no means easy to give a definitive explanation of what constitutes a dealer and what constitutes a collector. Many people would like to have the government believe that they are collectors because of the favorable capital gains treatment they would be able to take advantage of. But the following questions should be asked to help you determine what category you fall under. **Warning:** *Just because you answer several questions in a manner that indicates you are a collector does not mean that the IRS would, in fact, consider you to be one.*

• Do you buy and sell coins on a full-time basis?
• How much advertising do you do?
• How much time do you devote to the buying and selling of coins?
• What percentage of your income does your coin profit constitute?
• Are your coin sales continuous or sporadic?

- Do you pay sales tax on your coin purchases or do you use resale number?*
- Do you buy with the expectation of turning a profit?

There are, however, benefits to being a dealer. For example, business expenses are deductible. Again, consult a competent advisor in this area, such as a certified public accountant, in order to know what the answers mean in your particular case.

THE INCREASING GOVERNMENT PAPER TRAIL

The IRS is establishing ever-greater controls in an effort to enforce compliance. In the process, the government has the opportunity to find out some personal matters about you, such as your political beliefs. Furthermore, public documentation of valuable assets could make some people a target for litigation by private parties or victims of professional thieves.

Mark Skousen, writing in *Mark Skousen's Complete Guide to Financial Privacy,* gives the following advice, here slightly abridged:

- Discontinue using your present bank account for sensitive purchases. Make sensitive purchases with financial instruments such as money orders, and be sure to keep receipts for tax purposes.
- Restrict your use of credit cards to routine expenditures.
- Do not give your social security number unless required to do so by law.
- Store cash (or cash equivalent) at home for emergencies, with proof of where the cash came from.
- Try to avoid providing financial details and personal information when making investments.
- Consider an unlisted telephone number to ward off unwanted calls from high-pressure salesmen.
- Write to mail-order firms if you don't want your name on their mailing lists.
- Check your credit records to make sure the information is accurate.
- Apply for a passport to allow you travel flexibility.
- Maintain a low profile.
- Set up an *inter vivos* or living trust through your lawyer to preserve personal and financial privacy—as well as to avoid the costs of probate—at the time of your death.

---

* Sales tax on coins is required in most states. Legitimate dealers who are purchasing coins for resale, however, are exempt from paying the tax.

GIFTS AND ASSET TRANSFERS

The act of donating coins to nonprofit organizations, such as the American Numismatic Association, is often the source of a tax deduction to the donor as well as a source of revenue to the organization receiving the material.

In order to prevent an excessive deduction, the IRS has required since 1984 that the donor obtain a written, independent appraisal of the donated item. A copy of the appraisal report must be attached to the tax return. This applies to all tax returns filed in 1985 and beyond.

These requirements apply to gifts valued at over $5,000 (either singly or collectively). A sample of the American Numismatic Association's Deed of Gift is shown in figure 8-3.

However, an experienced attorney expressed the opinion that if the organization sells the donated material within two years of your having given it, then you must take as your deduction the value of the sale, even if it is lower than the appraisal.

Form **8300** (Rev.)
(Rev. January 1985)
Department of the Treasury
Internal Revenue Service

Report of Cash Payments Over $10,000
Received in a Trade or Business

OMB No. 1545-0892
Expires 12-31-85

Part I   **Individual or Organization for Whom This Transaction Was Completed**

Individual's last name	First name	M.I.	Social security number
Name of organization	Employer identification number	Passport number	Country
Number and street	Business or occupation	Alien registration number	Country

City	State	ZIP code	Country (if not U.S.)	Other identifying data (Specify)

Part II   **Identity of Individual Conducting the Transaction** (Complete only if an agent conducts a transaction for the person in Part I)

Last name	First name	M.I.	Social security number
Number and street	Passport number	Country	Alien registration number	Country

City	State	ZIP code	Country (if not U.S.)	Other identifying data (Specify)

Part III   **Description of Transaction and Method of Payment**

1 Amount of cash received $ **2** Amount in item 1 in $100 bills $

3 Nature of transaction   Description of property or service

- **a** ☐ personal property purchased
- **b** ☐ real property purchased
- **c** ☐ personal services provided
- **d** ☐ business services provided
- **e** ☐ intangible property purchased
- **f** ☐ debt obligation paid
- **g** ☐ exchange of cash
- **h** ☐ escrow or trust funds
- **i** ☐ other (specify) ▶

4 Method of payment by customer

- **a** ☐ paid with U.S. currency or coin
- **b** ☐ paid with foreign currency (describe)

5 Date paid

Part IV   **Business Reporting This Transaction**

Name of reporting business	Identification number (EIN or SSN)
Street address	Nature of your business

City	State	ZIP code

Under penalties of perjury, I declare that the information I have furnished above, to the best of my knowledge, is true, correct, and complete.

SIGN HERE ▶

(Authorized Signature—See Instructions)	(Title)	(Date)

For Paperwork Reduction Act Notice, see page 2.   Form **8300** (Rev. 1-85)

Fig. 8-2. Internal Revenue Service form 8300. Dealers are required by law to report cash transactions over $10,000 (or two or more related transactions that add up to over $10,000).

Museum of the American Numismatic Association
818 North Cascade Avenue
Colorado Springs, Colorado 80903
(303)632-2646

DEED OF GIFT

By these presents I (we) hereby irrevocably and unconditionally transfer to American Numismatic Association, its successors and assigns, by way of gift effective immediately, all my (our) right, title and interest in and to the following object(s) which I (we) own:

American Numismatic Association shall have absolute ownership of said property, including without limitation full powers of management, display, conservation and disposition as American Numismatic Association shall see fit in its absolute discretion and in the full exercise of its general corporate purposes.

Executed this _____ day of _____, 19_____

Name(s) _____   Signature(s) _____
                    Please Print

Address _____   _____

_____

We hereby accept the gift of said property and the delivery thereof.

AMERICAN NUMISMATIC ASSOCIATION

By _____   Title _____

_____
                    Date

Fig. 8-3. Deed of gift. This is the form used by the American Numismatic Association in accepting donated numismatic material. (Courtesy American Numismatic Association)

124

The Future

The technology is already in place for a dynamite future. But how we handle the development of the hobby, here and now, will shape the future. Waiting just ahead are electronic libraries, scientific grading of coins, instant electronic access to auction catalogs, inventory offerings, and market prices, as well as electronic publishing, video cassettes for numismatic education, electronic transmittal of photos, and new processes for preserving book papers for up to 600 years. The day of the computer is almost yesterday now. But Pac-Man will not munch away at the printed word.

Although there will be many technological advances in the near future, collectors must not forget the older traditions. The real reason for collecting must remain dominant: historical significance, beauty, and rarity of an object. These are adjuncts to life itself.

—Margo Russell, former editor, Coin World
(From an address before the "Coin Collector's Survival Conference," Detroit, July 29, 1984)

There are few industries other than the numismatic field in which the future assumes a role of such supreme importance. The future is a consideration in everything done by professional numismatists: every coin bought; every coin sold; every opinion rendered. The future is a time of potential richness and vitality, and the present is a time of potential opportunity. Although nobody can predict with certainty what tomorrow will bring, you owe it to yourself to think about what tomorrow *might* bring.

Many people are so caught up in the maze of yesterday's world that they can hardly envision what tomorrow could bring. Too many people think only about the here-and-now and are willing to let the future fall to happenstance.

125

Many people, too, look to the future in their own way and believe that there might not be a tomorrow. Some people are concerned about the large nuclear buildup and increasing political pressure between the superpowers and feel that the annihilation of humanity is imminent.

To some degree, your future is not in your hands. In a limited sense, the future of the numismatic market might be affected by what Robert Leuver or Ken Hallenbeck do as the heads of the American Numismatic Association; or by what Ed Reiter tells his readers about coins in *COINage* magazine; or by when Howard Ruff or Gary North sound the buy or sell signals; or by how young numismatist mentor Larry Gentile trains the next generation of collectors.

Do not be a person caught in the past. You need to think about what tomorrow will bring. *To a very great extent, your future is in your own hands.* Do not let the cries of the chronic nuclear worriers hinder your plans to build for future generations. Your children and your children's children are depending on you.

Never before in history have advances in technology so simplified everyday life. At the writing of this book in 1990, America is experiencing a technological renaissance. We are at the cutting edge of new technologies in every field. Every day brings a new scientific innovation. Although advances have not been made in permanently controlling monetary inflatings or balancing the United States budget, the private sector is taking giant leaps in the practical applications of complex technologies.

COMPUTERS AND THE RARE COIN INDUSTRY

Computers are assuming an increasingly greater role in the home. With each passing year, more and more people are joining the computer revolution. As the computer becomes an increasingly significant tool in everyday life, its uses in the rare coin industry multiply. The computer may well revolutionize the way coins are bought and sold.

Inventory and value calculation programs allow both collectors and investors to monitor and keep track of their investments closely. And the designing of these programs allows young computer whizzes to get a start in the numismatic field. One example is sixteen-year-old Rick Weerts, an Englewood, Florida, resident. Weerts has written the software for a comprehensive rare coin inventory tracking program now being offered through the mail. His software can be used on all IBM computers, most Apples, as well as on Radio Shack's TRS-80 (models 1, 2, and 3).

On the national level, American Teleprocessing Corporation's FACTS teletype system has for a number of years provided dealers with an electronically based trading system. Dealers use the teletype to buy and sell coins to each other. There are presently several hundred subscribers. Another popular system, also with several hundred subscribers, is Robert Sloat's CoinNet. Both systems offer spot gold and silver quotes.

A relatively new electronic coin network, Robert S. Riemer's Coin-Link (CLINK), allows both collectors and dealers to buy, sell, and trade coins with the assistance of any personal computer and a modem. The system can accommodate participants who want to trade coins "live" over the computer or leave numismatic buy and sell notices. Members are also invited to computer conferences with well-known numismatists. This network is expected to increase in popularity, for it is available to both collectors and dealers, and its services are reasonably priced.

The latest use of computers with coins is Bernard Rome's Teletrade. This system allows any coin trader with a touch-tone telephone to buy and sell certified coins. Rome's system is a live market and the consumer's equivalent of the American Numismatic Exchange. Rome utilizes state-of-the-art technology.

Plans are being made for the computerized grading of coins, although no known perfected system has yet been introduced. Any system in use today requires the assistance of an expert numismatist. However, great strides are being made in this area, and the prospect of computerized grading is a promising development that almost certainly looms on the horizon.

LASER TECHNOLOGY AND COIN GRADING

The introduction of the laser in consumer electronics has added a new dimension to home video. The video laser disc is universally recognized by video buffs and audiophiles as the finest home entertainment medium available.

But this exciting new technology has numerous uses in other fields, including medicine and, yes, *numismatics*. Many experts believe that a laser-based coin-grading system would be the most objective and accurate method possible of measuring gradational distinctions.

In an exclusive interview given for this book, Michael R. Fuljenz, director of numismatic services for the very large Metairie, Louisiana, firm of James U. Blanchard & Company, Inc., revealed that lasers are being closely considered for their applications in coin grading.

According to Fuljenz, the laser would be used in scanning a coin, and each mark would be carefully analyzed. The coin's viewing surface would be divided into subsections, and any mark on, for example, the cheek would be weighted more heavily than an identical mark in the field. The laser would move across the coin's grid-divided viewing surface, and the effect of the angular light would be synthesized as a component of the grade.

Space would have to be reserved on a satellite so that the information picked up by the laser could be transmitted to a major computer bank for proper interpretation.

Fuljenz said that the proposal, which was presented to his firm by a technology company, did have a number of drawbacks that make consideration of the laser as a coin-grading tool merely a theoretical concept at this time. Grading variables can be extremely complicated, and the laser might be less than perfectly accurate in determining how attractive a given coin is because of considerations relating to luster and toning. Furthermore, the system would have to be refined so that the laser would not, for example, mistake a white oxidation area for wear.

Fuljenz said that at the time he considered the proposal, the per-unit cost was in the millions of dollars. In addition, estimates that thirty coins per hour (or per operator) were the realistic number of coins that could be graded meant that the system would not pay for itself. The cost of the satellite space rental was extra, and general upkeep costs were determined to be prohibitive.

Nevertheless, many prominent numismatists remain optimistic that sometime in the future, as the technology continues to be refined, a laser coin-grading system will be a viable, cost-effective working reality.

CHANGES IN THE TAX LAWS

The Economic Recovery Act of 1981, which effectively disallowed coins from being placed in Keogh and IRA plans, has become the focus of an intensive reversal effort. ICTA is putting effort into once again making it a legal option for coins and other tangible assets to be placed in these plans.

Lawyer David L. Ganz feels that coins could be placed into Keoghs and IRAs a lot sooner than some believe, although Ganz expressed the opinion that the new allowance will probably not be the same as it was before, and that coins might only be allowed in such plans on a limited basis.

The reallowance of coins in Keoghs and IRAs would serve as a phenomenal stimulus to the numismatic market and might well cause a spectacular upward adjustment in many areas. Check with your accountant or tax advisor, and stay abreast of the developments of this potentially significant action.

Ganz is less optimistic about the capital gains rate, which he believes could be modified so that coin consumers might be taxed on profits at the full 35 percent rate. However, ICTA is also keeping close tabs on this matter, and if any negative governmental action seems likely, ICTA is expected to react immediately.

Other possible tax changes include raising the rate structure of coins donated to nonprofit organizations, such as the American Numismatic Association.

GOVERNMENTAL AND SELF-REGULATION

A number of people have argued that abuses in the rare coin industry are blatant and that some type of regulation, either by the industry or by the government (if the industry takes no steps to regulate itself), is a strong possibility. The industry is almost united in its belief that government regulation would be a burdensome, hampering element and that the coin field might not be able to continue to function profitably if the government were to intervene.

The following public service message was taken out in the August 21, 1985, *Coin World* by Stanley Apfelbaum, president of First Coinvestors, Inc., a coin investment firm that has since declared bankruptcy. Apfelbaum summarized the problems and wrote, in part:

> We must control the future of our industry by eliminating abuse. . . . The abuses practiced by telemarketing firms in numismatics are now approaching the abuses which were practiced in the gold and silver bullion contracts field. . . . The proliferation of these shops across the country is downright scary, and has moved me to start to think about this situation. . . . I am not optimistic that the short-term thinkers are going to voluntarily stop their abusive actions and I think it is time to take action and enact an industry-wide code of ethics. . . . Several very large bullion dealers, formerly rare coin people, have gone bad, taking with the demise of their firms tens of millions of dollars from trusting people. Following this came registration requirements for those who buy or sell bullion across the counter. . . . I believe that within a short time the numismatic

community may find that it is a regulated community, and that the fringe elements will have been removed or at least prosecuted by the proper authorities. I think that at the same time, as is the case in governmental intervention in private industry, the tone and the fun of collecting and investing and dealing and writing about rare coins will go the way of other industries that are over-regulated. . . . The fight by the various associations to fend off government regulation of bullion sales is patriotic and proof that one can fight City Hall and, at the very least, hold it to a standstill. But the numismatic industry itself has attracted to it a legion of hangers-on that may very well doom the industry to excoriating articles in national magazines, public scorn on television, and in the end, indictments and commission hearings and State and Federal prosecutions throughout the country. Almost every one of us in the industry has heard about the Mint State 65 coins being sold, which at their very best, are really AU 55s. The teletype machines abound, shamelessly, with advertisements for "slider" coins, or coins "close to MS 65." Advertisements in the numismatic papers and magazines purport to sell coins at twenty percent to fifty percent less than the Bid price in the *Coin Dealer Newsletter*. . . . I propose the establishment of an industry-wide telemarketing and grading consumer advocate commission to be run by a cross-section of dealers, collectors, writers and investors. . . . This body, acting with the cooperation of State and Federal authorities, can bring into line any and all companies and persons who cross the line of good business practices and fair ethics.

Apfelbaum's advertisement appeared at the same time a public debate was held on the subject between lawyer David Ganz and newsletter editor Maurice Rosen in conjunction with the A.N.A. convention in Baltimore, Maryland. Ganz and Rosen did not debate whether the industry should be regulated or not. Both agreed that the industry should be self-regulated, for at the very least, self-regulation will keep the government away and keep the market profitable for collector and investor alike.

Look for steps to continue to be taken by industry leaders to self-regulate.

Appendix

United States Rare Coin Types

The following listing is designed to assist you in the identification of United States coin Types and designs. The Type coin refers to an example of a particular type of coin, not a rare and sought-after date of that particular series. However, listed below are the regular issue dates of United States coins, including the rare dates.

It should be noted that many coins on this list have rarely been made mention of in the text. This is because some of these coins are *so old* that interest in them has waned and, thus, the collector base is not a solid one. Many early coins are either so high priced in high grades or so unobtainable (or both) that many collectors would not even try to complete a set of them. Nevertheless, there is a specialist somewhere willing to pay a premium for almost any rare United States coin in a high level of preservation.

Numismatic scholars believe that a different metallic content does not constitute a different coin Type and that different Types are only derived from different designs.

Half Cents
Liberty Cap, portrait left (1793 only)
Liberty Cap, portrait right (1794–7)
Draped Bust (1800–1808)
Classic Head (1809–36)
Braided Hair (1840–57)

Large Cents
Flowing Hair, chain reverse (1793 only)
Flowing Hair, wreath reverse (1793 only)
Liberty Cap (1793–6)
Draped Bust (1796–1807)
Classic Head (1808–14)
Coronet (1816–39)
Braided Hair (1840–57)

Small Cents
Flying Eagle (1857–8)
Indian, laurel wreath reverse, copper-nickel (1859 only)
Indian, shield reverse, copper-nickel (1860–64)
Indian, bronze (1864–1909)
Lincoln, V.D.B. reverse (1909 only)
Lincoln, wheat stalk reverse (1909–58)

Two-Cent Pieces
Shield obverse (1864–73)

Three-Cent Silver Pieces
No star lines (1851–3)
Three star lines (1854–8)
Two star lines (1859–73)

Three-Cent Nickel
Liberty obverse (1865–89)

Nickel Five-Cent Pieces
Shield, reverse rays (1866–7)
Shield, without reverse rays (1867–83)
Liberty Head, without "cents" on reverse (1883)
Liberty Head, with "cents" on reverse (1883–1913)
Buffalo reverse, complete mound (1913)
Buffalo reverse, lined platform (1913–38)
Jefferson nickel, Mint-mark above dome, silver (1942–5)

Half-Dimes
Flowing Hair (1794–5)
Draped Bust, small eagle on reverse (1796–7)
Draped Bust, large eagle on reverse (1800–1805)
Capped Bust (1829–37)
Liberty Seated, no stars on obverse (1837–8)
Liberty Seated, stars on obverse (1838–53)

Liberty Seated, stars and arrows by date on obverse (1853–5)
Liberty Seated, stars on obverse (1856–9)
Liberty Seated, legend on obverse (1860–73)

Dimes
Draped Bust, small eagle on reverse (1796–7)
Draped Bust, large eagle on reverse (1798–1807)
Capped Bust, large (1809–28)
Capped Bust, small (1828–37)
Liberty Seated, no stars on obverse (1837–8)
Liberty Seated, stars on obverse (1838–53)
Liberty Seated, stars and arrows at date on obverse (1853–5)
Liberty Seated, stars on obverse (1856–60)
Liberty Seated, legend on obverse (1860–73)
Liberty Seated, arrows at date (1873–4)
Liberty Seated, legend on obverse (1875–91)
Barber (1892–1916)
Mercury (1916–45)
Roosevelt, silver (1946–64)

Twenty-Cent Pieces
Liberty Seated (1875–8)

Quarter Dollars
Draped Bust, small eagle on reverse (1796 only)
Draped Bust, large eagle on reverse (1804–7)
Capped Bust, large (1815–28)
Capped Bust, small, without motto on reverse (1831–8)
Liberty Seated, no motto on reverse (1838–53)
Liberty Seated, arrows at date, rays around eagle on reverse (1853 only)
Liberty Seated, arrows at date, no reverse rays (1854–5)
Liberty Seated, without motto on reverse (1856–65)
Liberty Seated, motto on reverse (1866–73)
Liberty Seated, arrows at date (1873–4)
Liberty Seated, motto on reverse (1875–91)
Barber (1892–1916)
Standing Liberty, bare breast (1916–17)
Standing Liberty, covered breast (1917–30)
Washington Head, silver (1932–64)

Half-Dollars
Flowing Hair (1794–5)
Draped Bust, small eagle on reverse (1796–7)
Draped Bust, large eagle on reverse (1801–7)

Capped Bust, lettering on the edge (1807–36)
Capped Bust, reeded edge and "50 CENTS" on reverse (1836–7)
Capped Bust, reeded edge and "half dol." on reverse (1838–9)
Liberty Seated, without motto on reverse (1839–53)
Liberty Seated, arrows at date, rays around eagle on the reverse (1853 only)
Liberty Seated, arrows at date, no rays on the reverse (1854–5)
Liberty Seated, without motto on reverse (1856–65)
Liberty Seated, motto on reverse (1866–73)
Liberty Seated, arrows at date (1873–4)
Liberty Seated, motto on reverse (1875–91)
Barber (1892–1915)
Walking Liberty (1916–47)
Franklin (1948–63)
Kennedy, 90 percent silver (1964 only)

Dollars *(silver)*

Flowing Hair (1794–5)
Draped Bust, small eagle on reverse (1795–8)
Draped Bust, large eagle on reverse (1798–1804)
Gobrecht (1836–9)
Liberty Seated, without motto on reverse (1840–66)
Liberty Seated, motto on reverse (1866–73)
Trade (1873–85)*
Morgan (1878–1921)
Peace (1921–35)

Dollars *(gold)*

Liberty Head (1849–54)
Indian Head, small portrait (1854–6)
Indian Head, large portrait (1856–89)

Quarter-Eagles *($2.50 gold)*

Capped Bust, without stars on obverse (1796 only)
Capped Bust, stars on obverse (1796–1807)
Capped Bust, large (1808 only)
Capped Bust, portrait facing left (1821–34)
Classic Head (1834–9)
Coronet (1840–1907)
Indian (1908–29)

---

* The Trade dollar is the only United States coin that has been demonetized. In other words, it is not legal tender.

Three-Dollar Gold Pieces
Indian crowned LIBERTY (1854–89)

Half-Eagles *($5 gold)*
Capped Bust, small eagle (1795–8)
Capped Bust, large eagle (1795–1807)
Capped Draped Bust (1807–12)
Capped Head, portrait facing left (1813–29)
Capped Head, smaller diameter (1829–34)
Classic (1834–8)
Coronet, without motto on reverse (1839–66)
Coronet, motto on reverse (1866–1908)
Indian (1908–29)

Eagles *($10 gold)*
Capped Bust, small eagle on reverse (1795–7)
Capped Bust, large eagle on reverse (1797–1804)
Coronet, without motto on reverse (1838–66)
Coronet, motto on reverse (1866–1907)
Indian, without motto on reverse (1907–8)
Indian, motto on reverse (1908–33)

Double-Eagles *($20 gold)*
Liberty Head, without motto on reverse (1849–66)
Liberty Head, motto on reverse (1866–76)
Liberty Head, "DOLLARS" spelled out (1877–1907)
Saint-Gaudens, Roman numerals (1907 only)
Saint-Gaudens, Arabic numerals without motto on reverse (1907–8)
Saint-Gaudens, motto on reverse (1908–33)

Index

INVITATION FOR COMMENTS

The author welcomes comments about this book or the coin market. You can write to him at: Scott Travers Rare Coin Galleries, Inc., F.D.R. Box 1711, New York, NY 10150. Although there is no guarantee of a reply, the author makes an effort to read all correspondence sent to him.